CLASSICS IN EDUCATION

Lawrence A. Cremin, *General Editor*

☆ ☆ ☆

No. 1: THE REPUBLIC AND THE SCHOOL: Horace Mann on the Education of Free Men

No. 2: AMERICAN IDEAS ABOUT ADULT EDUCATION 1710-1951

SERIES PREFACE

The Classics in Education series presents the sources of the American educational heritage. As Mr. Grattan ably demonstrates in this volume, that heritage includes a great deal of wisdom about the values of adult education to individuals and to society as well. What knowledge is of most worth to adults? And how may they most economically and profitably obtain it? For more than two centuries thoughtful Americans have been wrestling with these questions. Their answers over the years are particularly relevant today, when upward of 8,000,000 men and women already attend some sort of formal adult course, and the number promises to rise significantly in the years ahead.

Lawrence A. Cremin

American Ideas about
ADULT EDUCATION
1710-1951

Edited, with an introduction and notes, by

C. HARTLEY GRATTAN

☆

CLASSICS IN

No. 2

EDUCATION

☆

BUREAU OF PUBLICATIONS
TEACHERS COLLEGE, COLUMBIA UNIVERSITY
NEW YORK

LIBRARY OF CONGRESS CATALOG CARD
NUMBER 59-9042

PRINTED IN THE UNITED STATES OF AMERICA
BY THE WILLIAM BYRD PRESS, INC.
RICHMOND, VA.

Contents

Introduction

THE DOCUMENTS presented in this book have been selected to illustrate characteristic thinking by Americans about adult education over a period of two and a half centuries. If it surprises some people that Americans have been thinking about the subject that long, that too will be a net gain, for the editor has hoped to reinforce a point he has made elsewhere and earlier, that adult education is an ancient human concern, not a strictly contemporary enthusiasm. The current outburst of enthusiasm for adult education is, as a matter of fact, but the latest of a long series. The editor's intention has been to select expositions of points of view that are closely related to actual undertakings in the field, that had a fairly impressive impact on adults over a significant period of time, rather than essays or speeches that, however valuable intrinsically, were nevertheless attempts to tour an alluring horizon with no concrete plan in mind for traveling toward it, or to influence the climate of opinion at the stratospheric level with no particular reference to specific action. Documents of the latter kind should, perhaps, be collected, but they have been neglected here. Hence when one reads what Lowell, Everett and Ticknor, Vincent or Meiklejohn had to say, it can be related to the institutions established, or to the utilization of the ideas in practice, and to the history that was made. To borrow a quotation that appealed to Lester Ward, a selection from whose writings appears in this book, "Application is the touchstone of all theory."

The editor may perhaps be permitted to refer, with proper modesty, to his book, *In Quest of Knowledge* (1955), for a sketch of the historical background of the documents here presented.

* * * * * * * * *

American adult education is closely connected with the widely shared American conviction that man is a creature who can be improved if he makes the effort and receives the proper and requisite encouragement and assistance. This general idea has been variously expressed and variously associated with other ideas and systems of ideas, especially those of a religious and political nature, and it early became involved in American thinking about economics, specifically about man as a producer and breadwinner. The idea has been a premise, openly avowed or not too subtly implicit, in discussions of adult education in America from 1710 to 1951 and beyond. It is both an expressed and unexpressed major premise in practically all American thinking about the subject. It appears in the very first selection in this book and it is found still going strong in the last. It is difficult to see how adult education could get along without it. Adult education is no field for pessimists about the potentialities of man.

Specifically it has long been assumed by adult educators that adults *can* learn. They have argued that old dogs can learn new tricks. If scientific underpinning for the position was not available until E. L. Thorndike published his *Adult Learning* in 1928, that is simply a remarkable and rather odd fact. The adult educators felt sure of it long before, otherwise they would not have tried to educate adults. Thorndike notably fortified their confidence. He turned a necessary assumption of adult educators into a scientifically verified fact.

But if the improvement of the individual man has been the focus of the effort, most of the writers here quoted have also taken into account the expected benefits to society that would follow from an improved man. They appear to have assumed that it was obvious that the quality of the men in a society determines the quality of the society and that a democratic society is peculiarly dependent for its success on the quality of the participating men. Apparently they saw no way of improving society without improving the men who are members of it. This is, of course, a reflection of an ancient dilemma: Should we concentrate on improving the institutional structure of society in the hope of making life better, or on improving man? The answer is, pretty plainly, that we should do both, but that either way it must be kept in mind that the root is man. If you let him escape your attention for very long you are, in a peculiarly disastrous sense, lost. By Americans, the consequences of improving man through education have long been assumed to be good both for the individual man and for the society in which he must function.

As a rule, in America, the improvement in man has been supposed to be made by increasing his knowledge and understanding in some respect or other, including knowledge and understanding of the vocational skills. The characteristic focus has been on the individual man, but the characteristic context for efforts on behalf of the individual has been a group. It should be kept in mind, however, that a part of the tradition we are discussing here is the practice of self-improvement, or a man working alone for his personal improvement. The early introduction of the group as the necessary unit is an indication that Americans very early concluded that only exceptional individuals could successfully go it alone. Benjamin Franklin pursued both courses, but the selection from him given here is chosen to illustrate his belief in the group approach. It is apparent, however, that shifting the emphasis from the individuals composing the group to the group as a thing-in-itself is a sad and late perversion of the American ideal, partly to be explained by misuse of the findings of the psychologists about the forces at work in group situations and the ways in which they can be directed to consolidate the group *qua* group. Larger wisdom would seem to dictate that increased understanding of how groups work should be used to make them work better for the benefit of the individual. This would be bringing new knowledge to the service of the invaluable and indispensable American tradition that it is the individual man who really counts, not only in God's sight, but in the sight of all who are concerned for the health of democratic society.

The United States will never be so rich that it can do without large increments of upstanding individuals in every generation.

It will be noticed that there is, in these selections, none of that characteristic overconcentration of interest on the cash returns to be expected by participants in adult education. That overconcentration, especially to be noted in vocational adult education, is readily to be accounted for by reference to the standard American criteria of success, money income and property holdings. It has wreaked much havoc and in the light of what the writers represented here have to say, must be reckoned a perversion of values. Reading through this book one cannot fail to be impressed by the fact that the classic emphasis, even when vocational education is involved (as in Peter Cooper's case), is upon the improvement of men in terms of secular knowledge, morals, or spiritual understanding, and only incidentally, or by implication, in terms of earning power. If earning power is mentioned, it is as an indispensable underpinning for the other values, not emphasized as something sufficient in itself to carry the whole load of justification for adult education. It therefore appears that those who today are arguing that American adult education needs a new dimension in the form of the elements of liberal education are really seeking to bring adult education more decisively into line with a firm and rich American tradition than it has been lately been—back into line with the tradition of improving the whole man, not merely the "hand" who will then earn more money.

The record as it is reflected in the following selections shows that American adult education has characteristically been thought of as a phase of an urgent social task known as "the diffusion of knowledge." The selection from Lester Ward is, in effect, a classic rationalization of this function. The editor does not recall a single occasion until very recent times when anybody alleged that he thought differently. Adult education has never pretended that it was alone responsible for the task; it has always recognized itself as but one instrumentality among many. For this reason also it has never attempted to define any particular segment of knowledge as uniquely its own; it has characteristically embraced a wide range of "disciplines" or subject-matters. It has an interest in both the "wisdom of the ages" and the "wisdom" of the strictly contemporary intellectual marketplace. There is simply no telling what wayfaring men may want to know and equally no telling what adult educators will offer to teach them. This is as it should be, for as an extremely important mechanism for the diffusion of knowledge, adult education cannot afford to assume the role of censor. What it always must do is to be sure that what it offers is truly knowledge. All too often one has one's doubts.

The Editor wishes to thank Mrs. Louise Smith, Assistant Librarian at The Fund for Adult Education for her skill and patience in gathering the books and documents from which the selections were made. This compilation was made possible by the financial assistance of The Fund for Adult Education.

C. Hartley Grattan

Katonah, New York
June 1958

AMERICAN IDEAS ABOUT ADULT EDUCATION 1710-1951

1

A Puritan as Adult Educator

COTTON MATHER

Cotton Mather (1663-1728), the archetypical "Puritan priest," son of the even more redoubtable Puritan, Increase Mather (1639-1723), was an incorrigible scribbler in the cause of righteousness. He was the author of four hundred separate works, one of which was Essays to Do Good *(1710). Barrett Wendell, in his biography of Cotton Mather, remarks that this book was "a work in which Mather insisted on a point that was always dear to him, the importance of combined, cooperative effort." From our present point of view Mather's book takes on especial significance as certainly one of the first, and perhaps the first, work bearing upon adult education published in America. Mather not only proposed, as the text quoted below shows, the formation of discussion groups but devised an ingenious scheme for keeping the discussion alive. That his device was well-conceived is shown by the fact that it was taken over and applied, with the questions rephrased, by Benjamin Franklin for use in* his *discussion group, The Junto* *(see page 18).*

A proper number of persons in a neighbourhood, whose hearts God hath inclined to do good, should form themselves into a society, to meet when and where they shall agree, and to consider "What are the disorders that we may observe rising among us; and what may be done, either by ourselves immediately, or by others through our advice, to suppress those disorders?" That they would procure, if they can, the presence of a minister with them; and every time they meet, present a prayer to the Lord to bless, direct, and prosper the design. That they would also procure, if possible, a justice of the peace, to be a member of the society. That half-yearly they choose two stewards, to dispatch the business and messages of the society, and manage the votes in it, who shall nominate their successors when their term is expired. That they would have a faithful treasurer, in whose hands their stock of charity may be deposited; and a clerk to keep a suitable record of their transactions and purposes; and, finally, that they carry on their whole design with as much modesty and silence as possible.

In a town furnished with several such societies, it has been usual for them all to meet together once a year, and keep a day of prayer; in which they have humbled themselves for doing so little good, and entreated the pardon of their unfruitfulness, through the blood of the great Sacrifice; and implored the blessing of Heaven on those essays to do good which they have made, the counsel and conduct of Heaven for their further attempts, and such influence of Heaven as may accomplish that reformation which it was not in their power to effect.

I will conclude this proposal by reciting those *points of consideration,* which may be read to the societies, at their meetings from time to time, with a proper pause after each of them, that any member may offer what he pleases upon it.

1. Is there any remarkable disorder in the place, which requires our endeavors and suppression of it? and, In what good, fair, likely way may we attempt it?

2. Is there any particular person, whose disorderly behaviour may be so scandalous, that it may be proper to send him our charitable admonition? or, Are there any contending persons whom we should exhort to quench their contentions?

3. Is there any particular service to the interests of religion, which we may conveniently request our ministers to take notice of?

4. Is there any thing which we may do well to mention and recommend to the magistrates, for the further promotion of good order?

5. Is there any sort of officers among us who are so unmindful of their duty, that we may properly remind them of it?

6. Can any further methods be devised that ignorance and wickedness may be chased from our people in general; and that domestic piety, in particular, may flourish among them?

7. Is there any instance of oppression or fraudulence, in the dealing of any sort of people, which may call for our efforts to present it in future?

8. Is there any matter to be humbly recommended to the legislative power, to be enacted into a law for the public benefit?

9. Do we know of any person languishing under heavy affliction, and what can we do for the succour of that afflicted neighbor?

10. Has any person a proposal to make, for the further advantage, assistance, and usefulness of this society?

2

A Founding Father as Adult Educator

BENJAMIN FRANKLIN

To quote Benjamin Franklin's account of The Junto and the closely related libraries may seem a desperate resort to the obvious, but the fact is that however familiar the Autobiography *has become, it is more commonly recalled that Franklin was a firm believer in the value of self-cultivation by private reading and study than that he was an inventor of, and participant in, group ventures in adult education. If American adult educators want to select a hero from among the fathers of the nation, their choice must inevitably fall upon Franklin; and since that is Franklin's true position in the history of adult education, continual reference to his own words is necessary that the spirit in which he approached the matter may not be lost from memory.*

I should have mentioned before, that, in the autumn of the preceding year, I had form'd most of my ingenious acquaintance into a club of mutual improvement, which we called the JUNTO; we met on Friday evenings. The rules that I drew up required that every member, in turn, should produce one or more queries on any point of Morals, Politics, or Natural Philosophy, to be discuss'd by the company; and once in three months produce and read an essay of his own writing, on any subject he pleased. Our debates were to be under the direction of a president, and to be conducted in the sincere spirit of inquiry after truth, without fondness for dispute, or desire of victory; and, to prevent warmth, all expressions of positiveness in opinions, or direct contradiction, were after some time made contraband, and prohibited under small pecuniary penalties.

About this time, our club meeting, not at a tavern, but in a little room of Mr. Grace's, set apart for that purpose, a proposition was made by me, that, since our books were often referr'd to in our disquisitions upon the queries, it might be convenient to us to have them altogether where we met, that upon occasion they might be consulted; and by thus clubbing our books to a common library, we should, while we lik'd to keep them together, have each of us the advantage of using the books of all the other members, which would be nearly as beneficial as if each owned the whole. It was lik'd and agreed to, and we fill'd one end of the room with such books as we could best spare. The number was not so great as we expected; and tho' they had been of great use, yet some inconveniences occurring for want of due care of them, the collection, after about a year, was separated, and each took his books home again.

And now I set on foot my first project of a public nature, that for a subscription library. I drew up the proposals, got them put into form by our great scrivener, Brockden, and, by the help of my friends in the Junto, procured fifty subscribers of forty shillings each to begin with, and ten shillings a year for fifty years, the term our company was to continue. We afterwards obtain'd a charter, the company being increased to one hundred: this was the mother of all the North American subscription libraries, now so numerous. It is become a great thing itself, and continually increasing. These libraries have improved the general conversation of the Americans, made the common tradesmen and farmers as intelligent as most gentlemen from other countries, and perhaps have contributed in some degree to the stand so generally made throughout the colonies in defense of their privileges.

3

A Mechanic on Adult Education

TIMOTHY CLAXTON

Timothy Claxton (1790–?) was an English mechanic of rural birth who went to town and caught the idea of a mechanics' institute out of the air of the time and tried to give it form and substance in England before he left that country for a tour of duty as chief mechanic of the oil-gas illuminating system of the Russian Czar's Ministry of War at St. Petersburg. In 1823 he arrived in America, direct from Russia, and shortly began experimenting again with the mechanics' institute idea, first at Methuen, Massachusetts, and then in Boston. He collaborated with Josiah Holbrook in establishing the Boston Mechanics' Lyceum in 1831, a variant of Holbrook's lyceum idea. Claxton left the United States in 1836 and returned to England. Only then did he meet with Dr. George Birkbeck and the mechanics' institute idea as Birkbeck had developed it. What became of Claxton in England we do not know beyond the fact that he established a shop, like one he kept in Boston, for making "apparatus" for scientific demonstrations in adult education classes. The following paper represents an effort by Claxton to sum up what he had learned from experience about adult education while in America.

On my arrival in Boston, my first object was to make inquiries respecting mechanics' societies; but I was surprised to learn that no society existed to which a mechanic could resort, and hear lectures on subjects calculated to aid him in his vocation. There had been some talk of building a mechanics' hall, &c.; but that project was abandoned. I conversed with several persons on the subject, who were willing to assist in forming a society for mutual improvement. I put a notice in a newspaper, stating where names would be received, and finally called a meeting, which was attended by nine persons; and a second, which was attended by only seven. At this meeting, it was determined to make the thing more popular, by advertising it in the daily papers, and hiring a hall in a central situation. The next meeting was held at Concert Hall, and was very well attended. The result was the formation of the Boston Mechanics' Institution. This was in 1826.

The society soon became popular, which induced others to follow the example thus set; so that it became evident that in Boston, as well as in other places, it only required a little exertion on the part of those who felt an interest in the subject, to induce at least a portion of its citizens to improve these advantages.

Finally, however, other societies of various kinds becoming numerous, the Institution became deprived of so large a share of its former patronage, that the receipts were found insufficient to defray the expenditures; and the lectures were discontinued (with a hope, however, of reviving them at some future time).

Being the first society in Boston, that introduced popular lectures on various branches of science, it would seem rather strange that it did not continue longer. The fact of the patronage being divided among a number of societies is not sufficient to account for its decline—it having made such an auspicious beginning, with a large number of members, and in addition to the regular assessments, a voluntary subscription having been set on foot soon after its organization, by which the liberal sum of about twelve hundred dollars was realized, and a collection of apparatus commenced. An act of incorporation was also obtained, and it had the appearance of a permanent institution; but the sequel shows that it was not conducted in a way to make it lasting.

As I have taken part in the management of this society from its formation, and have been very anxious for its success, I have, as a matter of course, formed my own ideas as to the causes of its decline. Not the least of these, I should say, was its unsocial character. A course of lectures, merely, during the winter, was all that the managers ever attempted: no library, reading room nor classes. A class on mechanical science was indeed formed, by members of the Institution, with the expectation that the managers would give it encouragement, and own it as a branch of the Institution; but they merely appointed a committee to consider the subject, with power to furnish a room for the class. They decided, however, that it was inexpedient; and some of the board thought it wrong to take the funds of the society for the purpose. The class might have supported itself, if persons could have been admitted who were not members of the Institution; but the rules of the class forbade it. In fact, the class adhered too closely to the rules of the parent for its own benefit; and was finally discontinued, for want of a little of that fostering care which the managers might have bestowed, with advantage to the parent institution, as well as to the class.

I took a very active part in this class, and had reason to expect that other classes would be formed on various subjects, which, while they enabled the members to make the most of the information received at the public lectures, by a more particular application, would have formed with the parent a bond of union not easily broken, and rendered some of the smaller societies since formed, unnecessary.

The plan of classes, in connection with a large institution is better, in some respects, than so many small, independent societies, which are generally of short duration, as the removal of one or two active members is often sufficient to discourage the others, and sometimes to break up the society. The classes, on the other hand, can be filled up from time to time, as long as they take an interest in the subject; and when that fails, other classes may be formed, on subjects in which an interest is taken. By the concentration of talent and energy, with the various facilities afforded by a popular institution, the classes can be conducted with more economy, and greater benefit, than can in general be secured by the smaller societies for mutual improvement. Still, I would not depreciate the latter, which will do much good, wherever they are carried on with the proper spirit; and there are many places where no other kind will succeed.

In my remarks on the management of the Institution, I disclaim the intention of imputing blame to any one. The gravest charge I am inclined to make, is that of error of judgment, in relation to the capacities of many persons among our youth and the humbler classes, for social and recreational enjoyment, as well as for self-improvement, which are found to exist, and to be easily developed, under suitable influences; and which are proved to be much more general than the inexperienced in these matters could have imagined.

So tenacious are mankind, in their adherence to ancient prejudices, that among the better informed, a small portion of aristocratic feeling is sufficient to close their eyes, so that they can neither see nor appreciate those favorable symptoms which are constantly developed. All my experience is in favor of these opinions, which are confirmed still more by what I have lately seen of the London Mechanics' Institution, and others of similar tendency.

In justice to the managers of the Boston Mechanics' Institution, I must acknowledge they were placed in a peculiar situation, requiring more tact, and a greater variety of auxiliary means, than the leading members were disposed to employ.

Among the many kindred societies that had adopted measures similar to those of this institution, may be named, as its greatest rival, the Massachusetts Charitable Mechanic Association. This was an old and powerful society, with plenty of funds; but the members were very careful how these funds were spent. For a long time, individual members had been trying to introduce something of an improving nature into the society; but when lectures were named, there were always a host against any such thing. The following has been related to me, as a specimen of the kind of opposition the liberal members had to contend with:

A proposition was made for a course of lectures on chemistry; on which a sensible member exclaimed—"What good will chemistry do us? If we want medicine, the cheapest way is to get it at an apothecary's shop." And strange to say—such remarks, the offspring of very contracted views, had more weight with the majority, than anything that could be urged in favor of the proposed measure.

The Association remained in this state when the Mechanics' Institution was formed; but the popularity of the latter soon brought the members of the former to their senses, and they actually voted one hundred dollars to a gentleman for a course of twelve lectures, which were delivered simultaneously with the second course given by the Institution. From that time, the Association has been progressing steadily; and there is some reason to hope that it will do much good in the end; for I have recently been informed that they are going on bravely in the work of improvement . . .

The Mechanics' Institution commenced on a liberal plan, paying twenty-five dollars for each of their lectures, which were so well attended that a repetition of them was practiced for some time, when forty dollars were paid for each lecture delivered twice. By such a course, the managers were enabled to procure several good lectures from regular professors, and to afford encouragement to other gentlemen of talent to prepare themselves. In this way, lectures were supplied for several years; and it is to be regretted that they could be no longer kept up. But it is some consolation to those who were the means of setting this intellectual and moral machinery in motion, in the capital of New England, to remember that it was effected by the Boston Mechanics' Institution, in the winter of 1826-1827.

In the summer of 1829, I took part in the formation of the Boston Lyceum. I was elected one of its curators, gave several lectures during the two first seasons, and assisted in conducting some of the classes. After that time, my attention to the society was relaxed, in some degree, by the formation of the Boston Mechanics' Lyceum, and my appointment as its president, which office I held from February 1831, until the termination of the fifth course of exercises, in 1835. These exercises consisted of lectures, debates, declamations, and occasionally, extemporaneous speaking—that is, speaking on a subject as soon as it is proposed. They were conducted on the mutual instruction principle, by the members alone, who were enabled to pursue this plan to advantage, after being well drilled to it in small classes.

This society has been often referred to, as a specimen of what mechanics and others might do for themselves, by suitable efforts. It has furnished speakers for other societies, engaged in various pursuits; and I might refer to one of the members, who used frequently to speak at temperance and other meetings, with good effect. One evening, I heard it remarked of him that he learned to speak at the Mechanics' Lyceum, which made me feel gratified, especially as this member had expressed a doubt of the success of the Lyceum, at its formation. I had been speaking encouragingly to the members, when he remarked, "That is all very well, if we can make it go." I devoted some of my best efforts to this society; and we *did* make it go—better, in fact, than many had anticipated.

4

The Lyceums: To Improve Schools and Diffuse Useful Knowledge

JOSIAH HOLBROOK

The originator of the idea of the lyceum was Josiah Holbrook (1788-1854) who devoted his life to education and most of it to adult education. A graduate of Yale in the class of 1810, his first educational enterprise was a private school in which academic study and farm labor were combined. He then—after returning to Yale to study under the redoubtable Benjamin Silliman (1779-1864), physicist, chemist and geologist, the father of popular science lecturing in America—toured as a lecturer to adult classes on geology. In 1826 he set out a suggestion for organizing adult education by establishing what he called "lyceums." By virtue of Holbrook's own indefatigable promotion and the close relation of the idea to the spirit of a time in which attendance at lectures was endemic, his scheme was widely adopted, especially in the northeast and middle west of the country. In the early stages there was good reason to suppose that the lyceum scheme would provide a nationwide framework for adult education, but this reasonable expectation was not realized. A considerable proportion of the energy behind the lyceums was drained off to the support of the movement for public schools and most of the rest went into promoting public lectures, at first by amateur lecturers, later by professionals. Holbrook's personal interest to the end of his life was promoting the study of geology by adult groups. He was drowned in Virginia while looking for specimens for his geological "cabinets." Our heritage from Holbrook is very complex, embracing as it does both what he intended and what he inadvertently promoted. He contributed largely and directly to the popularization of scientific knowledge (and incidentally to the establishment of scientific "collections"), established a base for lectures to adults, and provided a vehicle for mobilizing public sentiment behind the public schools. His was one of the earliest American careers in adult education. In 1829 the following discussion of Holbrook's idea was published in Boston.

This Institution consists of Town and County Lyceums, and measures are in progress to organize State Lyceums, and a GENERAL UNION of the whole.

TOWN LYCEUMS

A *town lyceum* is a voluntary association of individuals disposed to improve each other in useful knowledge, and to advance the interests of their schools. To gain the first object, they hold weekly or other stated meetings, for reading, conversation, discussion, illustrating the sciences, or other exercises designed for their mutual benefit; and, as it is found convenient, they collect a cabinet, consisting of apparatus for illustrating the sciences, books, minerals, plants, or other natural or artificial productions.

To advance the interests of schools, they furnish teachers with a room, apparatus, and other accommodations, for holding meetings, and conducting a course of exercises in relation to their schools, some of the eldest members of which, with other young persons, attend the meetings of Lyceums, where they are exercised and instructed in a manner fitted to their pursuits and wants. It is supposed that Lyceums may aid in furnishing schools with some simple apparatus, juvenile books or other articles, fitted to awaken an interest and communicate instruction to their members.

Town Lyceums have conducted their exercises in several different ways, to suit the wishes and acquirements of those who compose them. In some instances these exercises have consisted principally in reading interesting or useful articles from periodicals, a conversation on chemistry or other science, a biographical or historical sketch, communications of intelligence of improvements in education or the arts, or any other subject fitted for the entertainment or instruction of the members. The reading has frequently been accompanied or followed by questions, remarks, or conversation, by any disposed to introduce them.

In other meetings the sciences have been introduced by short and very familiar illustrations by the means of simple apparatus, six or eight, or perhaps ten or twelve, taking a part in the exercises of an evening. Under this plan of exercises, nearly all the members of the Lyceums which have adopted it have not only received, but communicated instruction.

In some Lyceums the instruction has been given principally in the form of lectures or dissertations, in which cases one or perhaps two have occupied the attention of the society during a sitting. The instruction given by lectures or dissertations, like that in a more mutual form, is intended to be of a familiar and practical character, that it may be brought within the comprehension of the most untutored minds.

Besides attending meetings of common interest to both sexes and all classes, females have conducted a course of mutual exercises among themselves, by spending together, during the summer, one afternoon in a week for reading, composition, and improvement in the various branches of an accomplished and enlightened education.

Teachers have also held meetings confined to themselves, in which they have introduced subjects and carried on exercises with particular reference to their schools. At these meetings they have had exercises in reading, giving an opportunity for critical remarks upon pronunciation, emphasis, inflection, modulation, and other points in good reading, all eminently calculated to improve them in this useful accomplishment. Exercises in grammar, composition, geography, arithmetic, illustrations in natural philosophy and chemistry, and sometimes discussions or dissertations upon the modes and principles of teaching, have been introduced at these meetings of teachers, and uniformly and immediately for the benefit of themselves and of the schools under their charge.

Some of the eldest members of the several schools in a town, with other young persons too far advanced or too much occupied to be benefited from the daily instruction of schools within their reach have, by the aid of professional teachers, clergymen, or other individuals (sometimes ladies) competent and disposed to guide them, carried on a course of weekly exercises, which have given them gradually, but certainly and permanently, a development and expansion of mind, and a refined and elevated taste.

Some of the advantages which have already arisen from the Lyceums which have gone into operation are the following, viz.:

1. The improvement of conversation. An immediate and uniform effect of a Lyceum, wherever it has been established and whatever the mode of conducting its exercises, is the introduction of good topics of conversation into the daily intercourse of families, neighbors, and friends, and that not among the members merely, but among all who come within the circle of its influence. Subjects of science, or other topics of useful knowledge, take the place of frivolous conversation or petty scandal, frequently indulged, and uniformly deplored, in our country villages. When it is considered that conversation is a constant, and an exhaustless source of information, either good or bad, in every town and among the whole race of mankind, it cannot but be evident that any measure which can give it an intellectual, moral, and of course an elevated character must confer a distinguished benefit upon society.

2. *Directing amusements.* Few subjects are more important, and none perhaps so much neglected, as amusements. Young people always have had, and, it is believed and hoped, they always will have, places of resort for social enjoyment. From the neglect of parents, and other persons of influence, to furnish them with occasions and opportunities to meet for exercises calculated for the instruction and improvement of each other, as well as for the enjoyment of social affections of a generous and elevated character, they resort to those calculated to corrupt and debase their minds, while they afford them no pleasures but those of the most grovelling character. Instead of having placed before them at their meetings books, apparatus, minerals, plants, and other objects calculated to acquaint them with the works and the laws of their Creator, and to lead them to admire the extent, the variety, the richness, and the grandeur of his creation, all designed and fitted for their immediate use and elevated enjoyment, they are presented with shelves of loaded decanters and sparkling glasses, so richly filled and so neatly arranged, and for *their* enjoyment, too, that to neglect them would be vulgar and unmanly. Experiments are of course made upon their contents, not, however, for their mutual entertainment in conversation, and reflection upon the works and the goodness of their Creator, but in the merry song, the vulgar wit, and the loud laugh. Parents and others to whom the rising generation look, and upon whom they depend for guidance and support, will you be offended at the question whether your children are most to blame for resorting to such places, and engaging in such exercises, or yourselves for neglecting to furnish them with better?

On the influence of amusements and conversation, always governing and partaking of the character of each other, and always determining the character of villages, communities, and the world, volumes might be written, but the occasion forbids enlarging.

3. *Saving of expense.* No principle in political econ-

omy is better established by experience than that a liberal support of religious and literary institutions is calculated to promote the pecuniary as well as the intellectual and moral prosperity of the community. Nor is there any mystery in this uniform result from the unerring hand of experiment. It has already been observed that young people must have occasions for social enjoyment and for recreation; and every one is familiar with the fact that the least useful and most pernicious amusements are the most expensive. The expense of a year's entertainment and instruction at the meetings and exercises of a Lyceum is from fifty cents to two dollars. The expense of one quarter's instruction in a dancing school, including extra clothes, pocket money, &c., cannot be estimated at less than ten dollars for each pupil. The expense of one evening's entertainment at a ball or assembly is from two to ten times the expense of a year's entertainment at the meetings of a Lyceum. Many young men have paid two dollars for a horse and chaise to ride upon the Sabbath, with too manly a spirit to mention it as an expense, who would be ready to confess themselves too poor to pay the same sum for a weekly course of the most useful instruction, through the year. Military exercises, which can hardly be considered in any other light than as amusements for young men, cost, upon an average, every one who engages in them in the Commonwealth of Massachusetts, not less than ten dollars annually. The average expense for a town is over two thousand dollars a year. All these amusements are attended with an expense of time which it is difficult to calculate, an expense of money for articles which it is impossible to name, and with an expense of intellects and morals which is truly appalling. These expenses it is the tendency of Lyceums to prevent.

4. Calling into use neglected libraries, and giving occasion for establishing new ones. It has been a subject of general regret that public libraries, after a short time, fall into neglect and disuse. Where a course of weekly or other stated exercises has been carried on in connection with or in the vicinity of a library, an occasion for this regret has never been known to exist; but, on the contrary, the demands immediately and uniformly created for books by the meetings and exercises of Lyceums have led to the enlargement of public libraries, and induced individuals to procure private libraries for their own use.

5. *Providing a seminary for teachers.* In the United States more than 50,000 daily teachers, and from 150 to 200,000 weekly teachers of Sabbath schools, are engaged in forming the character of the rising generation and moulding the destiny of our nation. Raising the qualifications of this responsible and important class of the community is an object of such vast moment to the prosperity of our country that for several years past it has been the frequent theme of conversation, addresses, sermons, and messages and speeches to legislatures. In many places this object has already been attained in a very efficient manner by weekly or other stated meetings of teachers for the improvement of each other. And at a very trifling expense for providing them with a room, apparatus, and other accommodations, for holding their meetings and conducting their exercises, every town in the United States may enable their teachers *immediately* and *constantly* to raise their own characters, and in such a way as *immediately* and *constantly* to raise the characters of their schools. If so, can any one conceive of a more powerful or more efficient seminary to qualify teachers than an institution which shall organize and direct a system of exercises by which they shall be enabled to qualify themselves, and that universally, immediately, and constantly?

6. *Benefiting academies.* Many academies, young ladies' seminaries, and other institutions of a similar character have been greatly benefited by the exercises of Lyceums. Regular courses of experimental lectures, procured from experienced teachers, and the weekly courses of mutual exercises conducted by Lyceums, have usually been offered as a gratuity, or at a small consideration, to the members of Academies and similar institutions for daily instruction. The opportunities of these pupils are

consequently increased, not only by providing them with a greater amount of instruction to be received from others, but by leading them to engage in new exercises to instruct themselves. In very many instances, members of Academies have interested others at the meeting of Lyceums; and, in affording an intellectual entertainment to their friends, they have received a tenfold benefit by instructing and improving themselves.

7. *Increasing the advantages and raising the character of district schools.* Public schools have been benefited, not only by the facilities offered by Lyceums for the improvement of their teachers, but by the opportunities they present directly to some of the eldest members of these schools to receive a course of weekly instruction of a higher character and under better advantages than can be given among the promiscuous assemblage of children, and the great variety of objects which these schools usually embrace. A weekly meeting of a few pupils from all the schools in a town, to be instructed and examined by several teachers, and by their parents or others interested in their welfare, acts almost with the rapidity and the power of electricity on all the teachers and all their schools. They immediately leave the dull monotonous circle in which they have been travelling for years, and commence an onward and upward course. Their energies are awakened and invigorated, their minds expanded, and they begin in earnest to lay broad and strong a foundation for their future characters and respectability.

8. *Compiling of town histories.* Several Lyceums have undertaken to procure histories of the towns where they are placed. In almost every town there remain a few of those patriots who purchased at so dear a rate the independence we now enjoy. And it would perhaps be difficult to determine to whom it would afford the purest and richest entertainment, to themselves in relating the tales of their wrongs, their battles, and their successes, or to their children and grandchildren in listening to them. But that it would afford a mutual entertainment to the old and young to hold a few meetings, to recount

and to learn the most interesting incidents in the history of the place of their residence or their birth, especially at this most interesting period in the history of our country, no one can deny or doubt. Nor can it be doubted that a historical sketch of every town would furnish interesting and important documents to be preserved for the generations that are to follow.

9. Town maps. A few Lyceums are taking measures to procure maps of their towns. To procure surveys for the purpose has been proposed as an exercise in the art of surveying to those who wish to acquire it. After a survey and draft are made, it is ascertained from artists that 200 lithographic prints can be procured for twenty-five dollars. And what family would not be willing to pay 12½ cents for a correct map of the town where they reside?

10. Agricultural and geological surveys. Many Lyceums have explored, thoroughly and minutely, the mineral productions, not only of the towns where they are placed, but of the surrounding country. Numerous interesting and useful minerals have been discovered, large collections have been made, and consequently new sources of industry and of wealth have been laid open, and the treasures of science have been enriched. And, when it is considered that the geology and mineralogy of our country are intimately connected with agriculture and internal improvements, the importance of having them fully and minutely explored must appear too great and too manifest to require one word to explain or enforce it. And, if time would permit, it might be easily shown that our resources in the mineral kingdom can be more fully and minutely explored, and the consequent knowledge placed more generally and directly in the possession of those who need it, through the agency of Lyceums than by any other method which can be devised.

11. State collections of minerals. Some of the States have commenced collections of minerals deposited in their capitols. When towns or counties are making surveys and collections for their own use, it will be easy to furnish specimens for a general collection, which might be arranged according to towns or geological divisions. These measures would furnish each State with a complete suite of its own minerals and a general collection of foreign specimens. Such collections would be useful, not only to science, but to agriculture and internal improvements, by placing before legislators and others specimens of their own productions, and a knowledge of their own resources in the mineral kingdom, by which industry would be encouraged and individual and public wealth and prosperity increased.

Such are some of the advantages which have already, either partially or fully, arisen from the mutual efforts of individuals in numerous towns for the improvement of themselves and the advancement of popular education.

CONSTITUTION

Many Lyceums have adopted the following or similar articles for their Constitution:

ARTICLE 1. The objects of the Lyceum are the improvement of its members in useful knowledge and the advancement of Popular Education.

ART. 2. To effect these objects, they will hold meetings for reading, conversation, discussions, dissertations, illustrating the sciences, or other exercises which shall be thought expedient, and, as it is found convenient, will procure a cabinet consisting of books, apparatus for illustrating the sciences, plants, minerals, and other natural or artificial productions.

ART. 3. Any person may be a Member of the Lyceum by paying into the treasury annually Two Dollars; and Twenty Dollars paid at any one time will entitle a person, his or her heirs or assigns, to one membership forever. Persons under eighteen years of age will be entitled to all the privileges of the Society, except voting, for one-half the annual sum above named.

ART. 4. The officers of this branch of the Lyceum shall be a President, Vice-President, Treasurer, Recording and Corresponding Secretaries, three or five Curators, and three Delegates, to be appointed by ballot on the first Wednesday of September annually.

ART. 5. The President, Vice-President, Treasurer, and Secretaries will perform the duties usually implied in those offices. The Curators will have charge of the cabinet and all other property of the Lyceum not appertaining to the treasury, and will be the general agents to do any business for the Society under their direction. The delegates will meet delegates from other branches of the Lyceum in this county semi-annually, to adopt regulations for their general and mutual benefit, or to take measures to introduce uniformity and improvements into common schools, and to diffuse useful and practical knowledge generally through the community, particularly to form and aid a BOARD OF EDUCATION.

ART. 6. To raise the standard of common education, and to benefit the juvenile members of the Lyceum, a portion of the books procured shall be fitted to young minds; and teachers of schools may be permitted to use for the benefit of their pupils who are members of the Lyceum the apparatus and minerals under such restrictions as the association shall prescribe.

ART. 7. The President or any five members will have power at any time to call a special meeting, which meeting shall be legal if notice shall be given according to the direction of the By-laws.

ART. 8. The Lyceum will adopt such Regulations and By-laws as shall be necessary for the management and use of the Cabinet, for holding meetings, or otherwise for their interest.

ART. 9. The foregoing articles may be altered or amended by vote of two-thirds present at any legal meeting, said alteration or amendment having been proposed at a meeting not less than four weeks previous to the one at which it is acted upon.

5

On Lectures for Moral and Intellectual Improvement

JOHN LOWELL, JR.

On April 1, 1835 John Lowell, Jr. (1799-1836), a merchant of Boston who was to die the next year in far-away Bombay, India, wrote a long letter to his cousin John A. Lowell elaborating a passage in his will of November 8, 1832 (the letter was in fact a codicil of the will) which provided for "the maintenance and support of public lectures to be delivered in said city of Boston upon Philosophy, Natural History, and the Arts and Sciences." The institutional expression of this benefaction is, of course, the Lowell Institute which survives to the present day with unimpaired vigor, a classic expression of the deepseated and long-persisting American belief in the efficacy of lectures as a means of moral and intellectual improvement. The letter, reproduced in greater part below, clearly reflects the quality and character of the thinking of John Lowell, Jr., about lectures and their proper management, matters upon which he had ample opportunity for forming views in the Boston of his day. Although it is now strongly felt that lectures are not enough truly to educate adults, there is little likelihood that lectures will ever be wholly abandoned by adult educators. It is well and profitable to be reminded of the intellectual climate out of which the belief in the efficacy of lectures originated in the United States; and also wise to take note of the fact that the impulse to provide support for adult education has deep roots in religion and morals. (It is worth noting, incidentally, that the present trustee of Lowell Institute is but the fourth in succession since 1836.)

My directions on the subject of said lectures are as follows:

1st in relation to the subjects. As the most certain and the most important part of true philosophy appears to me to be that which shows the connection between God's revelations and the knowledge of good and evil implanted by Him in our nature, I wish a course of lectures to be given on natural religion showing its conformity to that of our Saviour.

For the more perfect demonstration of the truth of those moral and religious precepts by which alone, as I believe, men can be secure of happiness in this world & that to come;

I wish a course of Lectures to be delivered on the historical and internal evidences in favor of Christianity: meaning by internal evidence arguments derived from the fulfillment of prophecies, or any other arguments not included under the head of natural religion.

I wish all disputed points of faith and ceremony to be avoided, and the attention of the lecturers to be directed to the Moral doctrines of the gospel: stating their opinion if they will, but not engaging in controversy even on the subject of the penalties of disobedience.

As the prosperity of my native land, New England, which is sterile and unproductive, must depend hereafter, as it has heretofore depended, 1st on the moral qualities and 2ndly on the intelligence and information of its inhabitants, I am desirous of trying to contribute towards their second object also; and I wish courses of lectures to be established on Physics and Chemistry with their application to the arts, also on Botany, Zoology, Geology and mineralogy, connected with their particular utility to man. After the establishment of these courses of lectures should disposable funds remain or in process of time be accumulated in the hands of the trustee; for there is a provision in my will touching a gradual accumulation of said funds; the said trustee may appoint courses of Lectures to be delivered on the literature and eloquence of our language and even on those of foreign nations if he sees fit, he may also from time to time establish lectures on any subject that in his opinion the wants and taste of the age may demand and he may abolish those already established, replacing them by others that he thinks more useful. But he shall not have power to abolish or to fail to establish those courses of lectures in favor of which I have herein expressed a wish or desire that they should be established neither shall he for the sake of other objects diminish the appropriation originally made in their favor.

2ndly. On the appointment and duties of Lecturers, as infidel opinions appear to me injurious to society and easily to insinuate themselves into a man's dissertations on any subject, however remote it may be from the subject of religion; no man ought to be appointed a lecturer who is not willing to declare and who does not previously declare his belief in the divine revelation of the Old and New Testaments, leaving the interpretation thereof to his own conscience. A lecturer may be taken on trial, but no one shall be appointed for a longer term than four years, nor from sentiments of delicacy ought his appointment to be renewed when he becomes incapable or superannuated.

Each lecturer ought to deliver two courses of Lectures on the subject for which he is appointed; one popular to be delivered three times a week, at an hour convenient for the public between the beginning of November and that of May; the other more abstruse, erudite and particular, to be delivered more frequently & at such times as may suit the convenience of those whose wish it is thoroughly to understand and examine the subject of the Lecturer. Every Lecturer, for whatever period appointed, shall be liable to be removed by the trustee for incapacity, neglect or omitting to fulfill his engagements. Previously to entering on his duties each Lecturer shall receive from the trustee an instrument in writing stating his compensation and the duties required of him.

It will of course be understood that by my directions on the subject of infidel ideas in the former part of this article, I am far from wishing either to express or encourage an intolerant spirit. I wish to do neither; but holding certain opinions that I believe beneficial to society I am desirous of promoting them, & I leave all judgment to God who alone discerns the right at all times.

Each Lecturer may be allowed by the trustee, whenever he may deem it expedient to allow, to receive a small sum from each scholar, who can afford it not exceeding the value of two bushels of wheat for the course of six months; but for the abstruse course only and not for the popular.

3rdly. On the appointment and duties of the trustee, each trustee shall appoint his own successor within a week after his accession to his office, in order that no failure of a regular nomination may take place. This appointment of his successor shall be made by means of a sealed instrument to be delivered to the trustees of the Boston Athenaeum, and which they shall open after the decease of the trustee who delivered it to them. The trustee may at any time, and as often as he sees fit, revoke his former appointment and take back the aforesaid instrument substituting another in its place. He may also nominate his successor in his will if he please so to do; and in case of a difference in the person nominated in the will and him who is nominated in the above mentioned instrument, the individual last nominated in point of time shall be his successor.

In selecting a successor the trustee shall always choose in preference to all others some male descendant of my Grandfather John Lowell, provided there be one who is competent to hold the office of trustee, and of the name of Lowell. The Compensation of the trustee shall be such reasonable sum, to be paid annually out of the income of the trust fund, as shall be approved by the trustees of the Boston Athenaeum for the time being. He shall keep an account of his management of the trust fund comformably to the provisions of my will and of the sums expended by him for the promotion of the objects of the trust. He shall also keep a record of all his proceedings touching the appointment of Lecturers & other objects connected with the trust. A copy of this account and of this record for the past year, shall on the first day of January be annually represented by him to the trustees of the Boston Athenaeum, who shall have authority to publish the same if they see fit.

The trustee shall require of every person attending the lectures to be neatly dressed and of an orderly behavior.

The popular courses always, and the other when practicable are designed for females as well as males.

When a lecturer is to be appointed, the trustee shall consult if it be practicable with two persons competently acquainted with the subject of the lectures proposed to be given, and with the persons who might be suitable candidates for the office, but he shall not be bound by the opinion of these persons, only if he differ from both of them he ought to insert the reason for his dissent in the record of his proceedings.

The trustee shall prescribe such rules touching the time, place and mode of delivering the various courses of lectures as he thinks fit, and may change them at his discretion.

The trustee may appropriate a portion of the income of the trust fund towards the gradual purchase of such philosophical apparatus and Books as may be absolutely necessary; and also if necessary towards the hire of lecture rooms, but he shall never appropriate any portion to the purchase of Lecture Rooms, of apparatus, of books or of any other property that does not yield a good and sufficient income.

It being my wish that the whole capital of the said fund should be always, the most productive possible;

and that its income should be appropriated as far as possible to the payment of efficient and able lecturers. I hope their offices will never become either a sinecure or a matter of favoritism.

6

On Libraries as Adult Education Institutions

EDWARD EVERETT AND GEORGE TICKNOR

Libraries have played a very important role in adult education both before and since the establishment of the Boston Public Library in 1852. The peculiar interest of the two letters which are partially quoted below is the directness of the connection the writers established between the proposed library they were discussing and adult education. In the long run the making of books available for circulation and reference has become disconnected from adult education in our thinking, and libraries are today not thought of as "in adult education" unless they also offer discussion courses, or lectures, or something of the sort. It is perhaps well to re-establish the old connection. Edward Everett and George Ticknor, who wrote these letters, thought that making books freely available would complete the structure of popular education. Perhaps we need to be cued to see public libraries in this light once again, for the conversion of the American adult public into a book-reading public would certainly be a long step forward in educational terms.

Edward Everett (1794-1865) was in his lifetime an immensely distinguished citizen of Boston: Unitarian clergyman, Ph.D. of Göttingen (the first American, indeed, to take a German doctorate), Profes-

sor of Greek Literature at Harvard and simultaneously editor of The North American Review, *Secretary of State under President Fillmore, Minister to England, President of Harvard, Senator from Massachusetts. He was the principal orator at Gettysburg when Abraham Lincoln delivered his brief but memorable address; and it symbolizes the transiency of eminence that nobody today ever recalls what Everett had to say on that celebrated occasion.*

George Ticknor (1791-1871), also a Bostonian, spent a quarter-century of his life as Professor of French, Spanish and belles-lettres at Harvard. He is still remembered among scholars of literature for his History of Spanish Literature *(1849).*

Everett's letter, dated June 7, 1851, was addressed to the Mayor of Boston and accompanied a rich gift of books. Ticknor's letter, dated July 14, 1851, was addressed to Everett as the leader of the movement for a city-supported public library. The two men later collaborated for many years in the management of the library that was established.

Edward Everett's Letter

The first principles of popular government require that the means of education should, as far as possible, be equally within the reach of the whole population . . . This however is the case only up to the age when School education is at an end. We provide our children with the elements of learning and science, and put it in their power by independent study and research to make further acquisitions of useful knowledge from books—but where are they to find the books in which it is contained? Here the noble principle of equality sadly fails. The sons of the wealthy alone have access to well-stored libraries; while those whose means do not allow them to purchase books are too often debarred from them at the moment when they would be most useful. We give them an elementary education, impart to them a taste and inspire them with an earnest desire for further attainment—which unite in making books a necessary of intellectual life—and then make no provision for supplying them.

For these reasons I cannot but think that a Public Library, well supplied with books in various departments of art and science, and open at all times for consultation and study to the citizens at large, is absolutely needed to make our admirable system of Public Education complete; and to continue in some good degree through life that happy equality of intellectual privileges, which now exist in our Schools, but terminates with them.

George Ticknor's Letter

I have seen with much gratification from time to time, within the last year, and particularly in your last letter on the subject, that you interest yourself in the establishment of a public library in Boston; I mean a library open to all the citizens, and from which all, under proper restrictions, can take out books. Such, at least, I understand to be your plan; and I have thought, more than once, that I would talk with you about it, but accident has prevented it. However, perhaps a letter is as good on all accounts, and better as a distinct memorandum of what I mean.

It has seemed to me, for many years, that such a free public library, if adapted to the wants of our people, would be the crowning glory of our public schools. But I think it important that it should be adapted to our peculiar character; that is, that it should come in at the end of our system of free instruction, and be fitted to continue and increase the effects of that system by the self-culture that results from reading.

The great obstacle to this with us is not—as it is in Prussia and elsewhere—a low condition of the mass of the people, condemning them, as soon as they escape from school, and often before it, to such severe labor, in order to procure the coarsest means of physical subsistence, that they have no leisure for intellectual culture, and soon lose all taste for it. Our difficulty is, to furnish means specially fitted to encourage a love for reading, to create an appetite for it, which the schools often fail to do, and then to adapt these means to its gratification. That an appetite for reading can be very widely excited is plain, from what the cheap publications of the last twenty years have accomplished, gradually raising the taste from such poor trash as the novels with which they began, up to the excellent and valuable works of all sorts which now flood the country, and are read by the middling classes everywhere, and in New England, I think, even by a majority of the people.

Now what seems to me to be wanted in Boston is, an apparatus that shall carry this taste for reading as deep as possible into society, assuming, what I believe to be true, that it can be carried deeper in our society than in any other in the world, because we are better fitted for it. To do this I would establish a library which, in its *main* department and purpose, should differ from all free libraries yet attempted. I mean one in which any popular books, tending to moral and intellectual improvement, should be furnished in such numbers of copies that many persons, if they desired it, could be reading the same work at the same time; in short, that not only the best books of all sorts, but the pleasant literature of the day, should be made accessible to the whole people at the only time when they care for it, i.e., when it is fresh and new. I would, therefore, continue to buy additional copies of any book of this class, almost as long as they should continue to be asked for, and thus, by following the popular taste—unless it should demand something injurious—create a real appetite for healthy general reading. This appetite, once formed, will take care of itself. It will, in the great majority of cases, demand better and better books; and can, I believe, by a little judicious help, rather than by any direct control or restraint, be carried much higher than is generally thought possible.

Nor would I, on this plan, neglect the establishment of a department for consultation, and for all the common purposes of public libraries, some of whose books, like encyclopaedias and dictionaries, should never be lent out, while others could be permitted to circulate; all on the shelves being accessible for reference as many hours in the day as possible, and always in the evening. This part of the library, I should hope, would be much increased by donations from public-spirited individuals, and individuals interested in the progress of knowledge, while, I think, the public treasury should provide for the more popular department.

Intimation of the want of such public facilities for reading are, I think, beginning to be given. In London I notice advertisements of some of the larger circulating libraries, that they purchase one and two hundred copies of all new and popular works; and in Boston, I am told, some of our own circulating libraries will purchase almost any new book, if the person asking for it will agree to pay double the usual fee for reading it; while in all, I think, several, and sometimes many copies of new and popular works are kept on hand for a time, and then sold, as the demand for them dies away.

Several years ago I proposed to Mr. Abbott Lawrence to move in favor of such a library in Boston; and, since that time, I have occasionally suggested it to other persons. In every case the idea has been well received; and the more I have thought of it and talked about it, the more I have been persuaded, that it is a plan easy to be reduced to practice, and one that would be followed by valuable results.

7

The Religious Motivation in Adult Education

PETER COOPER

In 1859 Peter Cooper (1791-1883), a New York inventor, manufacturer, and philanthropist executed a Deed of Trust establishing what has been known to subsequent generations as The Cooper Union for the Advancement of Science and Art and which has these many years stood astride the wavering line between formal and informal education for adults and young people in the sciences, the arts and the social sciences. Accompanying the Deed of Trust was a letter from Mr. Cooper, given below, setting out the background of his thinking about the Union (and offering some advice on its management). Once again, as in the instance of John Lowell's letter, the religious motivation for providing support for education comes vividly to attention. With the progressive secularization of education in America since the Civil War, this impulse has lost its force, or perhaps only become muted, or chiefly directed into particularistic channels. Today, at any rate, most thinking about adult education is done without reference to it. It is interesting to speculate on whether this represents progress or impoverishment; but beyond a doubt there is no possibility of understanding adult education historically without a clear comprehension of the religious motivation for its promotion.

It is to me a source of inexpressible pleasure, after so many years of continued effort, to place in your hands the title to all that piece and parcel of land bounded on the west by Fourth avenue, and on the north by Astor place, on the east by Third avenue, and on the south by Seventh street, with all the furniture, rents and income of every name and nature, to be forever devoted to the advancement of science and art, in their application to the varied and useful purposes of life.

The great object I desire to accomplish by the establishment of an institution devoted to the advancement of science and art, is to open the volume of nature by the light of truth—so unveiling the laws and methods of Deity, that the young may see the beauties of creation, enjoy its blessings, and learn to love the Being "from whom cometh every good and perfect gift."

My heart's desire is, that the rising generation may become so thoroughly acquainted with the works of nature, and the great *mystery of their own being, that they may see, feel, understand and know that there are immutable laws, designed in infinite wisdom, constantly operating for our good—so governing the destiny of worlds and men that it is our highest wisdom to live in strict conformity to these laws.*

My design is to establish this institution, in the hope that unnumbered youth will here receive the inspiration of truth in all its native power and beauty, and find in it a source of perpetual pleasure to spread its transforming influence throughout the world.

Believing *in* and hoping *for* such result, I desire to make this institution contribute in every way to aid the efforts of youth to acquire useful knowledge, and to find and fill that place in the community where their capacity and talents can be usefully employed with the greatest possible advantage to themselves and the community in which they live.

In order most effectually to aid and encourage the efforts of youth to obtain useful knowledge, I have provided the main floor of the large hall on the third story for a reading-room, literary exchange and scientific collections—the walls around that floor to be arranged for the reception of books, maps, paintings and other objects of interest. And when a sufficient collection of the works of art, science and nature can be obtained, I propose that glass cases shall be arranged around the walls of the gallery of the said room, forming alcoves around the entire floor for the preservation of the same. In the window spaces I propose to arrange such cosmoramic and other views as will exhibit in the clearest and most forcible light the true philosophy of life.

This philosophy will always show, when rightly understood and wisely applied, an inseparable connection between a course of vice and the misery that must inevitably follow. It will always show that "wisdom's ways are ways of pleasantness, and all her paths are peace."

To manifest the deep interest and sympathy I feel in all that can advance the happiness and better the condition of the female portion of the community, and especially of those who are dependent on honest labor for support, I desire the Trustees to appropriate two hundred and fifty dollars yearly to assist such pupils of the Female School of Design as shall, in their careful judgment, by their efforts and sacrifices in the performance of duty to parents or to those that Providence has made dependent on them for support, merit and require such aid. My reason for this requirement is, not so much to reward as to encourage the exercise of heroic virtues that often shine in the midst of the greatest suffering and obscurity without so much as being noticed by the passing throng.

In order to better the condition of woman and to widen the sphere of female employment, I have provided seven rooms to be forever devoted to a Female School of Design, and I desire the Trustees to appropriate out of the rents of the building fifteen hundred dollars annually towards meeting the expenses of said school.

It is the ardent wish of my heart that this school of design may be the means of raising to competence and comfort thousands of those that might otherwise struggle through a life of poverty and suffering.

It is also my desire that females belonging to the school of design shall have the use of one of the rooms not otherwise appropriated, for the purpose of holding meetings for the consideration and application of the useful sciences and arts to any of the various purposes calculated to improve and better their condition.

My hope is, to place this institution in the hands and under the control of men that will both know and feel the importance of forever devoting it, in the most effectual manner, to the moral, mental and physical improvement of the rising generation.

Desiring, as I do, to use every means to render this institution useful through all coming time, and believing that editors of the public press have it in their power to exert a greater influence on the community for good than any other class of men of equal number, it is therefore my sincere desire that editors be earnestly invited to become members of the society of arts to be connected with this institution. It is my desire that editors may at all times have correct information in relation to all matters in any way connected with this institution, believing that they, as a body, will gladly contribute their mighty influence to guard the avenues of scientific knowledge from all that could mar or prevent its influence from elevating the minds and bettering the hearts of the youth of our common country. I indulge the hope that the Trustees will use their utmost efforts to secure instructors for the institution of the highest moral worth, talents and capacity, fitting them to communicate a knowledge of science in its most lovely and inviting forms.

It is my design that the General Superintendent, under the direction of the Trustees, shall take all needful care of the building, and rent all unoccupied parts of the same.

The person to be appointed as a General Superintendent should be a man of known devotion to the improvement of the young. It will be his duty, not only to take charge of the building, but also to keep an office in the same, where persons may apply from all parts of the country for the services of young men and women of known character and qualifications to fill the various situations that may be open. It will be his duty to give, in the most kind and affectionate manner, such advice and counsel to all that may apply, as will most effectually promote their best interests through life.

Should any person ever be appointed a professor or superintendent who shall be found incompetent or unworthy of the trust, it is my earnest desire that such professor or superintendent shall be promptly removed.

It is my desire that students, on leaving the institution, shall receive a certificate setting forth their actual proficiency in any of the branches of science taught in the institution.

In order to encourage the young to improve and better their condition, I have provided for a continued course of lectures, discussions and recitations in the most useful and practical sciences, to be open and free to all that can bring a certificate of good moral character from parents, guardians or employers, and who will agree on their part to conform faithfully to all rules and regulations necessary to maintain the honor and usefulness of the institution.

Believing that instruction in the science and philosophy of a true republican government, formed, as it should be, of the people and for the people, in all its operations, is suited to the common wants of our nature, and absolutely necessary to preserve and secure the rights and liberties of all; that such a government, rightly understood and wisely administered, will most effectually stimulate industry and afford the best means possible to improve and elevate our race, by giving security and value to all forms of human labor; that it is on the right understanding and application of this science, based as it is on the golden rule, that eternal principle of truth and justice that unites the individual, the community, the state and the nation in one common purpose and interest, binding all to do unto others as they would that others should do unto them; thus deeply impressed with the great importance of instruction in this branch of science, I have provided that it shall be continually taught, as of pre-eminent importance to all the great interests of mankind.

My feelings, my desires, my hopes, embrace humanity throughout the world: and, if it were in my power, I would bring all mankind to see and feel that there is an Almighty power and beauty in goodness. I would gladly show to all, that goodness rises in every possible degree from the smallest act of kindness up to the Infinite of all good. My earnest desire is to make this building and institution contribute in every way possible to unite all in one common effort to improve each and every human being, seeing that we are bound up in one common destiny and by the laws of our being are made dependent for our happiness on the continued acts of kindness we receive from each other.

I desire that the students of this institution may have the privilege to occupy one of the large halls once in every month, for the purpose of a lecture to be delivered by one of their number to all students and such friends as they may think proper to invite.

The monthly lecturer shall be chosen from the body of the students by a majority vote, or a committee of the students selected for that purpose. The votes shall be counted and the name of the person chosen to deliver the lecture shall be announced, and a record made in a book to be provided for that purpose, to be the property of the institution. I desire that a record be kept of the names of the president, secretary and speaker —the subject treated, and the general course of remark. A president and secretary shall be chosen from the body of students by a majority vote, who shall preside at all meetings for lectures or other purposes, and whose term of service shall expire every three months, when another president and secretary shall be elected to take their places.

I require this frequent change, as I believe it to be a

very important part of the education of an American citizen to know how to preside with propriety over a deliberative assembly.

It is my desire, also, that the students shall have the use of one of the large rooms (to be assigned by the trustees) for the purpose of useful debate. I desire and deem it best to direct that all these lectures and debates shall be exclusive of theological and party questions, and shall have for their constant object the causes that operate around and within us, and the means necessary and most appropriate to remove the physical and moral evils that afflict our city, our country and humanity.

I desire that these lectures and debates shall always be delivered under a deep and abiding sense of the obligation that rests on all—first, to improve themselves, and then to impart to others a correct knowledge of that believed to be most important, and within man's power to communicate.

To aid the speakers, and those that hear, to profit by these lectures and debates, I hereby direct to have placed in the lecture-room, in a suitable position, full-length likenesses of Washington, Franklin, and Lafayette, with an expression of my sincere and anxious desire that all that behold them may remember that notwithstanding they are dead, they yet speak the language of truth and soberness.

Their lives and words of warning cannot be spurned and neglected without a terrible retribution on us and on our children—such a retribution as will cause their spirits to weep in sorrow over the crumbling ruins of all their brightest hopes for the improvement and renovation of the world.

Under a deep sense of the responsibility that rests on us, as a people, entrusted, as we are, with the greatest blessings that ever fell to the lot of man—the glorious yet fearful power of framing and carrying on the government of our choice—it becomes us to remember that this government will be good or evil in proportion as the people of our country become virtuous or vicious. We shall do well to cherish the precept that the righteous (or right doers) are recompensed in the earth, and much more the wicked and the sinner. It will be found that there is no possible escape from the correction of our Father who is in Heaven, who *"afflicts us not willingly but of necessity, for our profit; by His immutable law that rewards every man according to his works, whether they be good or whether they be evil."*

Desiring, as I do, that the students of this institution may become pre-eminent examples in the practice of all the virtues, I have determined to give them an opportunity to distinguish themselves for their good judgment by annually recommending to the Trustees for adoption, such rules and regulations as they, on mature reflection, shall believe to be necessary and proper, to preserve good morals and good order throughout their connection with this institution.

It is my desire, and I hereby ordain, that a strict conformity to rules deliberately formed by a vote of the majority of the students, and approved by the Trustees, shall forever be an indispensable requisite for continuing to enjoy the benefits of this institution. I now most earnestly entreat each and every one of the students of this institution, through all coming time, to whom I have entrusted this great responsibility of framing laws for the regulation of their conduct in their connection with the institution, and by which any of the members may lose its privileges, to remember how frail we are, and how liable to err when we come to sit in judgment on the faults of others, and how much the circumstances of our birth, our education, and the society and country where we have been born and brought up, have had to do in forming us and making us what we are. The power of these circumstances, when rightly understood, will be found to have formed the great lines of difference that mark the characters of the people of different countries and neighborhoods. And they constitute a good reason for the exercise of all our charity. It is these circumstances that our Creator has given us the power, in some measure, to control. This is the great garden that we are called upon to keep, and to subdue, and have dominion over, in order to find that everything in it *is very good,* that the right use and improvement of everything is a *virtue,* and the wrong or excessive use and perversion of everything, a *sin.* We should always remember that pride and selfishness have ever been the great enemies of mankind. Men, in all ages, have manifested a disposition to cover up their own faults, and to spread out and magnify the faults of others.

I trust that the students of this institution will do something to bear back the mighty torrent of evils now pressing on the world. I trust that here they will learn to overcome the evils of life with kindness and affection. I trust that here they will find that all true greatness consists in using all the powers they possess to do unto others as they would that others should do unto them; and in this way to become really great by becoming the servant of all.

These great blessings that have fallen to our lot as a people, are entrusted to our care for ourselves and for our posterity, and for the encouragement of suffering humanity throughout the world.

Feeling this great responsibility, I desire, by all that I can say and by all that I can do, to awaken in the minds of the rising generation an undying thirst for knowledge and *virtue,* in order that they may be able, by wise and honorable measures, to preserve the liberties we enjoy.

Fearing a possibility that my own religious opinions may be called in question, and by some be misunderstood or misrepresented, I feel it to be my duty, in all plainness and simplicity, to state the religious opinions that have taken an irresistible possession of my mind. At the same time, I require, by this instrument and expression of my will, that neither my own religious opinions, nor the religious opinions of any sect or party *whatever,* shall ever be *made* a *test* or *requirement,* in any *manner* or *form,* of or for *admission to,* or *continuance* to *enjoy* the *benefits* of *this institution.*

With this qualification, I would then impress, as with the last breath of my life, a fact which I believe to be the most exalting that the mind of man is permitted to contemplate, know, or understand—I mean the ennobling truth that there is one God and Father of all, who is over all and above all—who is forever blessed in the plenitude and fullness of his own infinite perfections; that this God is in very deed *our* Father; that he has created *us* in his own *image* and in his own *likeness;* that we may become one in *spirit,* and *co-workers* with *Him* in all that is good, great and glorious, for *time* and for *eternity.*

What can be more exalting than for the child to behold an infinite parent causing all the elements and essences of the universe to become his ministers—to organize, and individualize, and immortalize undying spirits, capable of knowing Him through an endless progress in knowledge and wisdom and power over the material universe forever; to feel that our Father in heaven has given to *us,* as *individuals, an immortality* and an endless growth, under laws so wise and good as never to require to be altered, amended, or revoked?

The life he has given us in his wisdom *is* an intelligent life—a life of accountability through our consciences, where every act becomes a part of ourselves, to live in our recollection forever.

I would impress the fact, that our Creator has used the best means possible in our formation or creation, and has given us the world, and all that in it is, with *life* and *breath,* and *all things richly to enjoy.* He has given all these blessings wrapt up in our capacity for an endless improvement and progress in the knowledge of our Creator, and in the power he has bestowed to receive and communicate happiness to all his intelligent creation. So that when we come really to know and feel that our God *is* love—to realize that He *is* indeed the Infinite of all that is good; when we come to see that he is drawing all the elements and activities of the universe into himself, and constantly elaborating them into higher forms of grandeur and beauty, and thus calling every intelligent creature to *wonder,* to *love,* and *adore forever.*

In this God I believe. I believe that he is a Spirit in whom we live, move and have our being; so that, if we ascend into the heavens, he is there, and if we descend into the depths of the earth, behold! he is there. I believe that he is filling immensity with his presence, comprehending all things within himself, and working all things after to good pleasure of his own will; that he is the same yesterday, to-day, and forever, and that *he changeth not.* I believe that God is love, and that love worketh no ill. I believe that *love must continue to use all its power through all eternity to give ever increasing happiness to all the creatures that he has made.* Such a God I trust I shall come to love with all the heart, soul, might, mind, and strength. I believe that God is so *in all* and *through all;* that what may be known of him is clearly seen, being understood by that which he has made, even his eternal power and Godhead: and that he *is* without variableness or shadow of turning. I believe that he will always work by wise and unalterable laws.

These laws, as far and as fast as they are comprehended by the faculties that he has given us, will be seen to be perfectly consistent and harmonious, and, like the stars in their orbits, "singing forever as they shine—*the hand that made us is divine.*"

With these views, I see as through a glass darkly, all the powers of the *universe* moving in obedience to immutable laws, guiding them onwards and upwards through all the various developments in the scale of being to a consciousness of God, and an accountability whereby we may show our love to God by the kindness and love that we manifest to the creatures that he has made. I believe that man, to be an accountable being, *must,* of *necessity,* be intelligent and free. He must feel and know that freedom and ability are given him to do what is required, before he can ever acknowledge it just or right that he should suffer for violating laws and requirements which he had neither the power nor the intelligence to understand or obey. Believing, as I do, that all the material creation centers in, and finds its culminating point in the organization, individualization, and immortalization of free intelligent beings—beings formed to rise through instinct into knowledge, and by knowledge into an accountability to an individual, and an undying conscience, and thence up to God—I believe mankind, throughout the world, require a religion founded on the highest idea that the human mind can form of all that is powerful, wise, pure and good.

Such a religion we have in those principles that guided the life of Christ, by which *he grew in knowledge* and in stature and in *favor* with *God* and *man,* from his youth up, and did always those things that are well pleasing to his Father and our Father; and by doing to others as he would that others should do to him, was enabled to overcome all evil; and although tempted in all points, as we are, yet he lived without sin. It will always be found to be our highest wisdom to follow his lovely example by avoiding all that is wrong, and by doing what good we can in the world.

Mankind will always require the great controlling principle of Christianity to be permanently fixed in the intellectual heart as the guide of life. We need a firm and unshaken belief in the inherent immortality of the soul; we need a solid conviction that God is love—love in action—love universal.

Such a belief in such a God will engage and secure our affections, and forever be to us the great reality of life. Our God will not then be to us a vaporish idea; on the contrary, he will be to us a God filling immensity with his presence and with the glory of his power. Were it possible for us to settle and establish this truth with unwavering certainty in the minds of men, temptation would be powerless. We should then see and feel that punishment inflicted for our good is as much the evidence of parental kindness as the blessings consequent on obedience to a righteous law. Every day shows me with more clearness that the great garden of the world is spread out before us filled with all the elements and inspirations of God, *"who is all and in all,"* constantly showing us that the same soil that can produce briars and thorns, and vex us in the land wherein we dwell, *can* be subdued by *wisdom,* and made to yield and supply our wants with nature's choicest fruits. How wonderful the wisdom that "connects in this, our greatest virtue, with our greatest bliss," "and makes our own bright prospect to be blest, the strongest motive to assist the rest." Every day shows me that if we are ever saved it must be by overcoming the world of *wrong within us* with such powers and faculties as God has given—to be the true light to enlighten every man that cometh into the world. There is no other *way* whereby we can be saved *but* by ceasing to do evil and learning to do *well.* To do this we need all the helps that we can find—we need to bear each other's burdens, and so fulfill the law of love. The life and teachings of Christ, showing God a father and the world of mankind our brethren, must forever stand pre-eminent over all forms of instruction, either ancient or modern. The loving spirit and principle that Christ manifested in *his* life and in his death, is the spirit that must finally reform the world, in the day when religion shall consist in the right actions and motives of our life, instead of a mere belief in the antiquated opinions of erring men. It was his gentle spirit—the spirit of an all-embracing charity—that went about the world, overcoming the evils of life with continued demonstrations of kindness and affection, and showed all that it is our privilege as well as duty to follow his example, and obey his precepts. It was this spirit that was in the world, and the world knew it not. It is still in the world, and it is our unhappiness that we know and feel so little of its influence on our hearts and lives. By following his precepts and example we cannot fail of a happy and useful life, a peaceful death, and a blessed immortality. I trust the time will come when religion will be divorced from superstition, and the light of science will develop the laws and methods of Deity, showing a great and glorious purpose shining through all the wonders of Almighty power, by which knowledge shall cover the earth as the waters cover the great deep, when men shall know and understand the things on which their happiness depends. We shall then comprehend something of the heights and depths and lengths and breadths of that knowledge and love of God which passes all understanding.

I have now placed in your hands the entire charge and property of this institution, and in order to further aid and facilitate the objects and purposes designed to be secured, I hereby authorize the Board of Control to draw on me at their pleasure for the sum of ten thousand dollars, as fast as the same can be wisely used to advance the interests of this institution.

Please accept my heartfelt assurance of sincere desire that under your care thousands of the youth of our country may throng its halls to learn those lessons of wisdom so much needed to guide the inexperience of youth amidst the dangers to which they are at all times exposed.

8

The Rationale of the Chautauqua Movement

JOHN H. VINCENT

John Heyle Vincent (1832-1920), a bishop of the Methodist Church from 1888, was the intellectual founder of the Chautauqua Assembly at Chautauqua, New York. Chautauqua was, in its heyday, one of the greatest of all American endeavors in adult education. Vincent was from his earliest days in the church keenly interested in the pedagogical side of the work, especially in the Sunday schools. He first established Chautauqua as a kind of residential summer normal school for Sunday-school teachers. This was in 1874. It was early discovered, however, that a wide variety of secular knowledge would be useful in setting forth "the mysteries of the spiritual kingdom" and the emphasis was soon switched to such knowledge and anybody who chose to do so could participate. Vincent had never in any case limited his efforts to Methodists. A highly complex organization was developed but the key segment of it, so far as adult education is concerned, was the Chautauqua Literary and Scientific Circle in which Vincent took a strong personal interest. This organization dispersed Chautauqua-style education, chiefly by careful, systematic, guided reading of books and other materials, much of it specially prepared for the Circle, plus formal examinations, to hundreds of ad hoc *groups and to isolated individuals in small towns throughout the nation. Aside from visits students might make to Chautauqua in the summer vacation season, all contact was by mail. What Bishop Vincent had in mind he set out in a valuable book called* The Chautauqua Movement *(1886), from which the following representative passage has been selected.*

The task I have taken upon myself is to tell, in a simple way, the story of Chautauqua—a story of to-day; without romantic, heroic, or tragic element; a story of the people; a story in which the scholars will be interested, because the scholars are a part of the people; a story in which the rich and the refined will be interested —the rich who are truly refined, and the refined whether rich or poor—because they believe in the brotherhood of the race and in its high destiny, and are proud to account themselves a part of it.

I shall make no effort to excite the pity of the wealthy and the learned for the poor and the illiterate—class for class, upper for lower. Chautauqua is not one of the "associated charities," nor is it a department of "home missions." It comes alike to the door of want and of wealth, with proffered blessings for both, and is as likely to gain entrance at one door as at the other. It deals with matters which, by the order of an impartial Providence, belong to "all classes and conditions of men." The full-orbed "Chautauqua idea" must awaken in all genuine souls a fresh enthusiasm in true living, and bring rich and poor, learned and unlearned, into neighborship and comradeship, helpful and honorable to both.

Education, once the peculiar privilege of the few, must in our best earthly estate become the valued possession of the many. It is a natural and inalienable right of human souls. The gift of imagination, of memory, of reason, of invention, of constructive and executive power, carries with it both prerogative and obligation.

No man dare with impunity surrender, as to himself, this endowment, nor deny to his neighbor the right and obligation which it involves. Given, intellectual potentiality; required, intellectual discipline and power. The law holds among leaders of thought, teachers and lawmakers; among nobles and the favorites of fortune. It holds no less among the lowly—the plebeians and the peasants of society.

Diversity in the direction of talent, and difference in degree, together with inequalities of social condition, may modify the demand upon the individual for culture and service; but the utter neglect of intellectual capacity is criminal, whether it be by menial or millionnaire. It involves a wrong to self, to the family, to the state: to self, since it leaves him blind whom God created to enjoy the light; to the family since it turns him into a physical or commercial machine whom God appointed to be companion and comforter; to the state, since it makes him a mere figurehead—whether of clay or gold —whom God intended to be a counsellor and helper, and to "have dominion" according to the measure of his power. No man has a right to neglect his personal education, whether he be prince or ploughboy, broker or hod-carrier. He needs knowledge, and the wisdom which makes knowledge available. Where the power lies, there rests responsibility for its use. Circumstances seem to favor the prince, and to be against the ploughboy; but, after all, the latter, overcoming adverse conditions, may acquire an education worth a great deal more to the world than that of the prince with his opportunities. Struggle against what men call fate brings power. One hour of study every day, with heroic purpose, may prove more valuable to the student than five hours a day of easy memorizing and reciting. The prince may complete his course in a few years, and, having "finished," graduate. The ploughboy, moving slowly, may require four times the number of years to cover the same ground; but that length of time may be an advantage to the humble student. It may require greater concentration when he does study; and the long hours of manual labor may be enriched by thought, and thus may knowledge gain a firmer hold, and its vitalizing power be increased.

Chautauqua has a work to do for college graduates. It enters protest against the suspension of intellectual effort when the compulsory *régime* of the recitation-room has been remitted—a fault so common and so pernicious that college men themselves frequently bring into disrepute the college system. Intellectual activity must be continuous in order to promote intellectual health and efficiency. College life is the vestibule to a great temple. He who crosses its pavement, and reads the inscriptions on its doors, but goes no farther, might as well never have entered the campus at all. Too many suspend literary pursuit when the diploma is won, and the world of business opens before them. Chautauqua provides, for such as these, incentives to a personal review of the entire college curriculum in a series of English readings. It urges them to prosecute advanced courses of study, and suggests a plan by which college prestige and power may be used in helping less favored neighbors who desire education. This last class is large. It is made up of eager minds who need direction and encouragement. They would ask questions, and gratefully accept assistance, if college graduates would simply place themselves within reach.

Chautauqua has therefore a message and a mission for the times. It exalts education—the mental, social, moral, and religious cultures of all who have mental, social, moral, and religious faculties; of all, everywhere, without exception. It aims to promote a combination of the old domestic, religious, educational, and industrial agencies; to take people on all sides of their natures, and cultivate them symmetrically, making men, women, and children everywhere more affectionate and sympathetic as members of a family; more conscientious and reverent, as worshippers together of the true God; more intelligent and thoughtful as students in a universe of ideas; and more industrious, economical, just, and generous, as members of society in a work-a-day world. The theory of Chautauqua is that life is one, and that religion belongs everywhere. Our people, young and old, should consider educational advantages as so many religious opportunities. Every day should be sacred. The schoolhouse should be God's house. There should be no break between sabbaths. The cable of divine motive should stretch through seven days, touching with its sanctifying power every hour of every day.

Kitchen work, farm work, shop work, as well as school work, are divine. They hide rare pearls in their rough shells. They are means of discipline in the highest qualities of character, and through them come some of the greatest and mightiest energies from the heavens. People should be guarded against the baleful heresy, that, when they leave the hour of song, prayer, and revival power, and go to homely service in shop or field, they are imperilling spiritual life, as though only so-called sacred services could conserve it.

We need an alliance and a hearty co-operation of Home, Pulpit, School, and Shop—an alliance consecrated to universal culture for young and old; for all the days and weeks of all the years; for all the varied faculties of the soul, and in all the possible relations of life.

Chautauqua teaches that each of these institutions embodies and represents an idea, and that every man needs in his own life these representative ideas—the home idea of mutual love and tenderness; the church idea of reverence and conscientiousness; the school ideal of personal culture; and the shop idea of diligence, economy, and mutual help. The young and the old need these things. The rich and the poor need them. Capital and labor need them. The educated and the illiterate need them. Chautauqua says therefore: Give them to the people. Hold up high standards of attainment. Show the learned their limitations, and the illiterate their possibilities. Chautauqua pleads for a universal education; for plans of reading and study; for all legitimate enticements and incitements to ambition; for all necessary adaptations as to time and topics; for ideal associations which shall at once excite the imagination, and set the heart aglow. Chautauqua stretches over the land a magnificent temple, broad as the continent, lofty as the heavens, into which homes, churches, schools, and shops may build themselves as parts of a splendid university in which people of all ages and conditions may be enrolled as students. It says: Unify such eager and various multitudes. Let them read the same books, think along the same lines, sing the same songs, observe the same sacred days—days consecrated to the delights of a lofty intellectual and spiritual life. Let the course of prescribed reading be broad and comprehensive; limited in its first general survey of the wide world of knowledge; opening out into special courses, according to the reader's development, taste, and opportunity. Show people out of school what wonders people out of school may accomplish. Show people no longer young, that the mind reaches its maturity long after the school-days end, and that some of the best intellectual and literary labor is performed in and beyond middle life. College halls are not the only places for prosecuting courses of study. College facilities are not the only opportunities for securing an education. A college is possible in everyday life if one choose to use it; a college in house, shop, street, farm, market, for rich and poor, the curriculum of which runs through the whole of life; a college that trains men and women everywhere to read and think and talk and do; and to read, think, talk, and do, with a purpose; and that purpose, that they may *be:* a college that trains indolent people to work with their own hands; that trains people who work with their hands, to work also with their brains,—to think in their work, to think for their work, and to make other people work and think.

A plan of this kind, simple in its provisions, limited in its requirements, accepted by adults, prosecuted with firm purpose, appealing to the imagination and to the conscience, must work miracles, intellectual, social, and religious, in household, neighborhood, and nation. And this is the "Chautauqua Idea"; and the idea in active operation is the *Chautauqua* of which I write.

Its benefits are manifold and obvious. It brings parents into fuller sympathy with their children, at the time when sympathy is most needed—sympathy with them in their educational aims, sympathy with them in lines of reading and study.

It helps parents to help the teachers of their children, preparing infants under school age to make a good beginning; inciting and assisting the children who have entered school, to do good work in preparation and recitation; protecting them against the peculiar temptations of playground and class-room; holding them to the end of the high-school course; inspiring them to seek the higher education of the college, or to pursue after-school courses of reading and study at home.

So general a scheme of education must increase the refining and ennobling influence of home life, promoting self-control and dignity of deportment, mutual respect and affection, a laudable family pride, and true social ambition; giving the whole house an air of refinement; touching with artistic skill floors, walls, and windows; finding the right place and the right light for the right picture; putting the right book on shelf and table; furnishing a wider range of topics for home conversation; crowding out frivolity and gossip; removing sources of unrest and discontent at home; making evenings there more agreeable than life on the street; creating a real independence of the outside world, and making one's own house the centre of the whole world of science, literature, art, and society. Windows open out through every wall; and beyond vines, trees, and garden, the inmates see the old world of history, the new world of science, the rich world of literature, the royal world of art. And through skylights they look up and see the world of God—his love and holiness, and the boundless life to which he invites us. And thus they all in that household learn, that, seen aright, all realms of knowledge, both past and present, are flooded with the light of God.

Popular education through the Chautauqua scheme increases the value of the pulpit by putting more knowledge, thoughtfulness, and appreciation into the pew, and encouraging the preacher to give his best thought in his best way.

It must put more good sense into popular religious utterances, so that the talk of the prayer-meeting will be sobered by wisdom and directed by tact, thus gaining in its influence over cultivated people, and especially over the young people of high-school and lecture-hall. It must enable everybody more accurately to measure the worth and the limitations of science, and must cause them to fear far less the dogmatism of pseudo-scientists concerning religious facts and doctrines.

Such popular education must increase the power of the people in politics, augmenting the independent vote which makes party leaders cautious where lack of conscience would make them careless concerning truth and honesty.

It must tend to a better understanding between the classes of society, causing the poor to honor wealth won by honest ways of work, by skill and economy; to despise wealth and winners of wealth, when greed and trickery gather the gold; to honor knowledge and a taste for knowledge, whether it be found clad in fine linen or in linsey-woolsey; to hate with resolute and righteous hatred all sham and shoddy, all arrogance and pretentiousness; to avoid struggles between capital and labor, and to promote, in all possible ways, the glorious brotherhood of honesty, sympathy and culture—a culture that addresses itself to all sides of a man's nature.

Under the auspices of this great Chautauqua "everyday college," you may imagine the soliloquy of a woman more than forty-five years of age. She says:

"I am busy with many duties—household cares or shop work. I have something to do all the time. There seems no end to calls, toils, worry, and weariness. In kitchen, parlor, farm, or factory, something is to be done.

"I am old—that is, older than I once was. Don't let

us talk about that. Gray hairs? No, you cannot find any gray hairs in my head—or, can you? Never mind. The heart's young, and it's nobody's business how old the bones are.

"I am going to college! Never mind about thirty years, or fifty, or seventy: I am going to college. Harvard? No, nor Yale, nor Boston, nor Middletown, nor Evanston, nor Wellesley. I don't want to mix with a lot of reckless boys, or ambitious girls, just now. I have enough of them at home or in the neighborhood. I am going to college, my own college, in my own house, taking my own time; turning the years into a college term; turning my kitchen, sitting-room, and parlor into college-halls, recitation-rooms, and laboratory. What a *campus* I have! green fields and forests, streams and mountain ranges, stretching out to the sunset. What a dome surmounts my college! vast space, blue background, billowy clouds, resplendent stars! What professors I have, in books! immortal books of history and science and art, books of poetry, fiction, and fact.

"In my college are enrolled the names of glorious men and women who never enjoyed any other college—Shakspere, Benjamin Franklin, Washington Irving, John G. Whittier, Horace Greeley, Abraham Lincoln, and hosts of others who went to their own college, and wrought out their own education, as I will do in 'my college.' I can never be what they were; but I can be something, and can make the world better, and children happier, and life nobler, because of the feeble efforts I put forth to get a better education.

"I am going to college! I want to improve all my talents. I have intellect. I intend to develop and enrich it. I must know more. I must love to know. I must know more, for the sake of larger influence over others for their good—children, servants, neighbors, church associates. God has given me at least one talent. I ought to improve it. I will improve it.

"I am going to college! I am a 'child of a King,' and have a right to my inheritance. 'All things are yours.' Well, I want to take up my property in stars and flowers, and in the knowledge men have gathered about my royal Father's kingdom. Astronomers, bring me what you have discovered in the outlying domains of my Father's universe! Geologists, tell me the story you have learned from the rocky pages of the earth, concerning the beginnings and the development of the planet I live on. Thus I intend to lay hold of all the treasure-seekers and teachers and high priests of nature and literature and art, and bid them bring the truth they hold, my Father's truth, *my* truth, and place the goodly inheritance at my feet. 'Whatsoever things are true . . . think on these things.' I am going to college!

" 'Where am I going?' I shall stay at home, and construct a college there. My house—small, poorly furnished (never mind)—is my college centre. My neighbors, the richest of them and the poorest, the most humble and ignorant, and the most scholarly, shall be my professors. I will ask questions about everything, and of everybody, till I find out what I want to know. Some of the stupidest people can tell me something, and when I draw them out I do them good. Getting, I can give.

"And don't talk to me about age. Let the poet answer your raven cry":

But why, you ask me, shall this tale be told
To men grown old or who are growing old?
It is too late! Ah! nothing is too late
Till the tired heart shall cease to palpitate.
Cato learned Greek at eighty; Sophocles
Wrote his grand Œdipus, *and Simonides*
Bore off the prize of verse from his compeers,
When each had numbered more than fourscore years;
And Theophrastus at fourscore and ten
Had but begun his Characters of Men;
Chaucer, at Woodstock with the nightingales,
At sixty wrote the Canterbury Tales;
Goethe at Weimar, toiling to the last,
Completed Faust *when eighty years were past.*
These are, indeed, exceptions; but they show
How far the gulf-stream of our youth may flow

Into the arctic regions of our lives,
When little else than life itself survives.
Shall we, then, idly sit us down and say:
The night hath come: it is no longer day?
The night hath not yet come: we are not quite
Cut off from labor by the failing light.
Something remains for us to do or dare;
Even the oldest tree some fruit may bear;
For age is opportunity no less
Than youth, though in another dress;
And as the evening twilight fades away,
The sky is filled with stars invisible by day.

The entire Chautauqua movement is based upon the following propositions:

1. The whole of life is a school, with educating agencies and influences all the while at work, from the earliest moment to the day of death. These agencies and influences should be wisely and continuously applied by and in behalf of each individual, through life, according to circumstances, capacities, and conditions.

2. The true basis of education is religious. The fear of the Lord is the beginning of wisdom—the recognition of the Divine existence, and of his claims upon us as moral beings; the unity and brotherhood of the race, with all that brotherhood involves; harmony with the Divine character as the ideal of life for time and eternity; and the pursuit and use of all science in personal culture, the increase of reverent love for God, and of affectionate self-sacrifice and labor for the well-being of man.

3. All knowledge, religious or secular, is sacred to him who reverently surrenders himself to God, that he may become like God, according to the divinely appointed processes for building character. And he has a right to all attainments and enjoyments in the realm of knowledge, for the possession of which he has capacity and opportunity. Science, travel, literature, the works of art, the glories of nature—all things are his who is one with God. This law applies to the poor and lowly, as well as

to the rich and so-called "favored classes" of society. It gives lofty ideals to lowly life, and transforms humble homes into places of aspiration and blessedness.

4. In mature life, beyond the limits of the usual school period, the intellect is at its best for purposes of reading, reflection, and production. While the training of the schools may discipline the juvenile mind, and thus give it an advantage as its powers mature, the discipline of every-day life, in solving problems of existence, support, and business, gives a certain advantage to the so-called uneducated mind during the middle period of life. Between the ages of twenty and eighty lie a person's best intellectual and educational opportunities; and he needs direction, encouragement, and assistance, in order to use them most effectively.

5. Early lack of culture, felt by full-grown people, begets a certain exaltation of its value and desirability, and a craving for its possession. This craving creates intellectual susceptibility and receptivity, and renders the more easy the acqusition of knowledge. Mere verbal memory may be less efficient in these adult years; but the power of reasoning, and of utilizing knowledge for practical results, is much greater than in the early years.

6. The necessity for wise direction, assistance, and encouragement of this mature intellectual power and desire is as great as in the period of youth and of school life. Therefore grown people need courses of study outlined, books for reading indicated, questions answered, associations formed,. and all the conditions guaranteed which tend to promote hope, confidence, ambition, and strong purpose.

7. Where a mature mind desires to use its energies and opportunities to the maximum of its possibility, and to do thorough intellectual work of the most exacting sort, the influence of the best teachers may be brought to bear upon him by frequent correspondence, including questions, answers praxes, theses, and final written examinations of the most exhaustive and crucial character. To such persistent purpose and faithful effort, after rigid testing, there should come the testimonials

and honors in diploma and degree, to which any student anywhere else, or at any other period of his life, would be entitled.

8. The advantage of mental attrition [i.e., interaction] by personal recitation and conversation is a large factor in the schools. This advantage may be enjoyed by voluntary associations, local circles, contact with resident scholars, occasional attendance upon special lectures, and class recitations in local high-schools, seminaries and colleges, and at summer schools and assemblies.

These are some of the fundamental thoughts on which the Chautauqua movement is based. It is a school for people out of school who can no longer attend school—a college for one's own home; and leads to the dedication of every-day life to educational purposes.

9

On Teaching by Correspondence

W. R. HARPER

Although adult education by correspondence was first tried out in the United States as early as 1873, it did not become well established as a part of the educational scene and of American folklore (as an integral factor in the Alger-boy complex of notions) until the early nineties. William Rainey Harper (1856-1906), chiefly remembered now as the intellectual founder of the University of Chicago, early experimented with instruction by mail, especially of Baptist ministers in theological subjects, and as he was on the staff of Chautauqua as professor of Greek and Latin in the School of Languages, and since the Chautauqua Literary and Scientific Circle was based upon instruction by mail, it was natural that Harper should have been asked by Bishop Vincent to make an analysis of the method. The following paper, apparently written in the mid-eighties, brilliantly presents Harper's conclusions. Probably no better case was ever made. It is interesting indeed, in the light of all this, that Harper's University of Chicago still advertises instruction by mail in the national magazines.

Four questions may be considered: (1) What *is* the correspondence-system of teaching? (2) What disadvantages attend this system, as compared with oral teaching? (3) What advantages, if any, does the correspondence-system have over oral teaching? (4) What results have thus far been accomplished in the line of teaching by correspondence? In the statements made, special reference is had to the teaching of langauges.

I. *What Is the Correspondence-System?*

A brief explanation of the plan of study by correspondence is first in order.

1. An *instruction-sheet* is mailed to the student each week. This instruction-sheet (a) assigns the tasks which are to be performed—e.g., the chapters of the text to be translated, the sections in the grammar to be learned; (b) indicates an order of work which the student is required to follow; (c) offers suggestions on points in the lesson which are liable to be misunderstood; (d) furnishes special assistance wherever such assistance is deemed necessary; (e) marks out a specified amount of review-work; (f) contains an examination-paper which the student, after having prepared the lesson, is required to write out. The instruction-sheet is intended, therefore, to guide and help the student just as an oral teacher would guide and help him.

2. The *examination-paper* is so constructed, that, in order to its preparation for criticism, one must have prepared before hand most thoroughly the lesson on which it is based. An examination-paper on Caesar, for example, requires of the student (a) the translation of certain chapters into English; (b) the translation into Latin of a list of English sentences based on the Latin which has just been translated; (c) the explanation of the more important constructions, with the grammatical reference for each construction; (d) the placing of forms; (e) the change to "direct discourse" of a corresponding passage in "indirect discourse"; (f) the explanation of geographical and historical allusions; (g) the statement of grammatical principles, etc., etc.

3. In the *recitation-paper* submitted to the instructor, besides writing out the matter called for in the *examination-paper,* the student asks such questions, and notes

such difficulties, as may have presented themselves to him in his study of the lesson. This recitation-paper is promptly returned with all errors corrected, and questions answered; and with special suggestions, suited to each individual case.

In this manner each lesson of the course is assigned and studied; and the results of the study submitted to the instructor for correction, criticism, and suggestion.

From this it will be seen that the correspondence-teacher must be painstaking, patient, sympathetic, and *alive;* and that the correspondence-pupil must be earnest, ambitious, appreciative, and likewise *alive*. Whatever a *dead* teacher may accomplish in the classroom, he can do nothing by correspondence; and if a student lacking the qualities just named undertake work by correspondence, one of two things will happen: either he will acquire these qualities, and succeed; or he will remain as he was at the beginning, and fail. The man who does the work at all, must do it well.

II. *The Disadvantages under Which the Correspondence-Student Works*

There are, I frankly confess, some disadvantages under which the correspondence-student works, and it is only fair to consider them.

1. The personal magnetism of an instructor is often felt by pupils for years after they have ceased to come in contact with him. Some teachers—and it is an occasion of regret that the number of such is not larger—exert upon the students an influence for good which cannot be estimated. Such influence the correspondence-student does not feel; such stimulus he does not receive.

2. In the recitation-room, there is a certain class-spirit, and a certain spirit of emulation, which tend to elevate the student, to quicken and to dignify him. This, of course, is for the most part lacking in the correspondence-work.

3. An earnest, conscientious teacher, in whatever department he may work, will unconsciously furnish information, impart methods of work, let drop suggestions,

which are not to be found in text-books. Under the inspiration of the class-room he will lead his pupils by paths which he himself never trod before. All this, the correspondence-student loses.

4. Ordinarily the student makes one hundred and sixty to one hundred and eighty recitations in a given study during the year. The correspondence-student makes but forty.

5. There is a drudgery in the work of writing out long lessons, which some regard as almost unendurable. This is in sharp contrast with the freedom and pleasure with which others make an oral recitation.

6. There is necessarily a large amount of irregularity in the correspondence-work. The interruptions are, in the very nature of the case, quite numerous; and after such interruptions there inevitably comes discouragement. This is a most serious difficulty.

7. The correspondence-student is not under the eye of an instructor; the temptation to be dishonest is always at hand. He is more likely to use illegitimate helps, and to misuse legitimate ones, than is he who must produce the results of his work in the presence of his comrades and at a moment's notice.

8. Whatever the common opinion may be, the requirements of the correspondence-system are of so exacting and rigid a nature as to prevent some from completing the work, who would certainly be able to pass through the course of study in many of our so-called colleges. This may or may not be a disadvantage of the correspondence-system, according to the point of view taken.

These difficulties, it is true, exist; but some things may be said, which will, at least slightly, modify their force.

1. If personal stimulus furnished by the teacher is absolutely necessary to good results on the part of the student, then two-thirds of the oral instruction given is valueless; for it is safe to assert that two out of three teachers exert no such influence upon their pupils, their work being purely mechanical.

2. Is it true that this personal magnetism, this personal influence, cannot be conveyed by writing? Have words spoken, or words written, produced the greater effect? Have not many of us received greater inspiration from personal letters than from words uttered by mouth? Are there not among our best friends those whom we have never seen, whose voice we have never heard, whose words have reached us only by letter?

In my experience with students by correspondence, brief as it has been, I can refer to hundreds of men who have acknowledged the stimulus and inspiration received by letters in the course of their study.

3. Class-spirit is not wholly lacking. The student knows that he is a member of a class which probably numbers hundreds, the members of which live in every State and Territory and even in foreign lands. Is there not inspiration in this fact? He knows, also, that every recitation-paper is graded, that his progress is very closely watched, that his classmates are pushing on notwithstanding difficulties and obstacles as great as he is called to meet. Is there not stimulus in all this?

4. Only forty recitations a year are required; yet each of these forty demands the preparation and the work of three or four oral recitations; and were the number less than forty, and the amount accomplished less, the fact that the student prepares his lesson knowing that he must *recite the whole of it,* and that he must recite it by writing, goes far to make up in quality what perhaps in quantity might be lacking.

5. The drudgery is very great, but not so great as many imagine. Besides, those to whom the work seems so onerous are those of whom such work as a matter of discipline should be required.

6. While in correspondence-work it is true that interruptions and consequent discouragements are more likely to occur, it is equally true (a) that this evil is largely mitigated by the fact that the average correspondence-student is thirty years of age, and therefore old enough to overcome the bad effect of such interruptions; (b) that a rigid system of reviews helps greatly,

also, to counterbalance this evil; and (c) that, while work lost from sickness or other cause is never really made up in the ordinary class, in the correspondence-class no work is lost, the student being required to begin at the point reached when the interruption took place.

7. After all, dishonesty in correspondence-work is more easily detected than in an oral recitation. And, besides, what is easier than so to construct the examination-paper, in each case, that at least in a large portion of the work no direct aid may possibly be obtained?

8. It is proper in this connection to consider the following points: (a) No one has ever thought of substituting the correspondence-system for the oral; the latter is conceded to be superior, and only those are advised to study by correspondence who cannot in any way obtain oral instruction. (b) The fact that the large proportion of correspondence-students are voluntary workers removes many difficulties which under other circumstances might exist. (c) What the student loses in his correspondence-work, he may easily gain by attending Summer Schools, which, indeed, are intended to supplement the correspondence-work.

III. *What Advantages Does the Correspondence-System Have?*

While it is freely conceded that there are disadvantages attending the correspondence-system, it is confidently claimed that this system has some advantages over other systems. Our space will scarcely permit any thing more than a bare mention of these:

1. By the correspondence-student, compelled to express every thought *in writing,* there is gained what the student reciting orally does not so easily acquire—the habit of *exact statement.*

2. Of the correspondence-student, compelled to state *in writing* his conception of a principle, or his translation of a paragraph, there is demanded a greater *accuracy of knowledge* than is necessary for an ordinary oral recitation.

3. While each student, in an oral recitation, recites

only one-tenth, one-thirtieth, or one-sixtieth of the lesson assigned, each correspondence-student recites the entire lesson, however long it may be. In four oral recitations, each student in a class of thirty recites eight minutes: in the preparation of a single recitation-paper, the correspondence-student spends at least two hours, aside from the previous work of preparing the lesson. The oral student must recite rapidly, often hurriedly: the correspondence-student works out his recitation-paper slowly, thoughtfully.

4. The correspondence-student, given all *necessary* assistance, but compelled to obtain every thing else for himself, or write out his questions and wait for the written answer, is led to investigate, to be independent in his study, and to have a confidence in the results of his own investigation which the student who has constant recourse to his instructor does not have.

5. If a written examination is a more thorough test of a student's knowledge of a given subject, surely a written recitation is not, in respect to *thoroughness,* inferior to an oral one. The correspondence-system requires of its students more thorough preparation of the lesson assigned, a more thorough recitation of it, and, in a word, a more thorough knowledge of the subject treated of in that lesson.

6. A prime requisite in good teaching is the ability to assign the proper lesson. Many excellent teachers fail at this point. The lesson is too long, or too short; the ground to be covered is not definitely indicated; the method of work is not clearly stated, etc., etc. The correspondence-lesson, since it is generally in printed form, is prepared with the greatest care. No part of it is given out hurriedly. It is the result of hours of careful study and calculation. If it is too long to be prepared within six days, the student is allowed a longer time; if it can be prepared within a less time, the student can take up the next lesson. Nothing could be more definite than this lesson, for it is assigned with a minuteness of detail which to some doubtless seems superfluous, but which in the case of others is absolutely essential.

7. Finally, whatever may be the relative merits of the two systems, it is clear to every one who thinks, that there are thousands of men and women unable to avail themselves of oral assistance, who, nevertheless, are eager to study. It is surely an advantage of the correspondence-system, that it can aid this large class, who otherwise would have no help, and would make no progress.

These are some of the advantages of the correspondence-system. But is any one to suppose that there exists, in the mind of those especially interested in this system, a desire to have it take the place of oral instruction? Is the one in any sense a rival of the other? I wish here to record, in answer to these questions, a most emphatic *No*. What is the fact? *Only those persons are encouraged to study by correspondence, or, indeed, admitted to such study, who because of age, poverty, occupation, situation, or some other good reason, cannot avail themselves of oral instruction.* Away, therefore, with all baseless and foolish prejudice in this matter! The correspondence-system would not, if it could, supplant oral instruction, or be regarded as its substitute. There is a field for each which the other cannot fill. Let each do its proper work.

IV. *What Has Been Accomplished Thus Far in the Line of Correspondence-Work?*

In the strict sense of the term, the correspondence-system has been in use only four or five years. This time has been sufficient, however, to enable us to note a few practical results:

1. It has already helped thousands of men toward a knowledge of certain subjects, which otherwise they would not have had.

2. There are to-day many thousands of men already convinced of the feasibility of the system, who are but waiting for the moment to arrive at which they shall begin. Educators in all lines are beginning to appreciate the possibilities of this system.

3. Institutions have been established, chief among which stands the CHAUTAUQUA COLLEGE OF LIB-

ERAL ARTS, through whose influence the system will be more fully developed, and rendered capable of accomplishing still greater good.

I venture, in closing this very brief and imperfect presentation, to make two statements; one an assertion based on large experience, the other a prediction based on strong conviction:

1. The student who has prepared a certain number of lessons in the correspondence-school knows more of the subject treated in those lessons, and knows it better, than the student who has covered the same ground in the class-room.

2. The day is coming when the work done by correspondence will be greater in amount than that done in the class-rooms of our academies and colleges; when the students who shall recite by correspondence will far outnumber those who make oral recitations.

10

Education for All: Problem of the 20th Century

THOMAS DAVIDSON

Thomas Davidson (1840-1900), born in Scotland and educated there, was considered one of the twelve most learned men of his time. He taught at one time or another in educational institutions in England, Canada and the United States, edited a learned journal in the field of education, and wrote extensively, particularly on the history of education, especially on Greek education. He was reckoned a perceptive critic of the education of his time and, when opportunity offered, a fruitful innovator in it. During the latter part of his life, which was chiefly spent in and around New York City, he engaged in private teaching and was largely concerned, therefore, with adult education. He was hostile to the university extension of his day because he considered it merely an extension of a defective university education. On the one hand he maintained a "Summer School of the Cultural Sciences" at his farm in the Adirondack Mountains which was chiefly attended by members of the intelligentsia (and which was lovingly described by William James in an essay now available in Memoirs and Studies), *and on the other hand he helped found a school for workers in New York City. The latter was to have two intimately related aspects: it was to be a college* *of culture and also a polytechnic for vocational training. Davidson saw clearly that one's life must have a strong vocational underpinning to give it economic stability, but he insisted that vocational competence should be accompanied by a sharing in the cultural heritage of mankind. His scheme was never fully developed, for he died early in the history of its application, but it went far enough to have become a memorable experiment both in actuality and potentiality. It foundered as much because of the absence of his powerful leadership as anything else, thus demonstrating that adult education depends heavily upon the quality of the available leadership. The following essay,* prepared originally as a lecture which was delivered in 1898, contains some of Davidson's most seminal ideas.*

A *free* life is the only life worthy of a human being. That which is not free is not responsible, and that which is not responsible is not moral. In other words, freedom is the condition of morality. That is simple enough.

Now, freedom, taken in its broadest sense, is conditioned by several things, such as health of body, wealth, and, above all, education. It is obvious enough that, however wealthy and cultured a man may be, if he has not health, his freedom will be sadly curtailed in its exercise. Nor is it less obvious that, if a man is destitute of wealth, and has to spend his entire time in obtaining the bare necessaries of life, he is to all intents and purposes a slave to his body. Lastly, it is clear enough that the uneducated man, however well endowed with health and wealth, is a slave. In the first place, he is a slave to other people's opinions, as every one must be who fails to think for himself. He who acts upon the thought of another is practically that other's slave. This we see daily in the political world, where the great body of the

* From *The Education of Wage Earners,* by Thomas Davidson. Edited by C. M. Bakewell. Reprinted by permission of Ginn and Company.

people, on account of their ignorance, are deprived of their rights, and often of other things, by selfish men who have received a good education. In the second place, he is continually faced by circumstances, the bearing of which he does not understand, and hence is compelled either not to act at all, or else to act in the perilous dark. Worst of all he is cooped up in a pitiful, beggarly world of facts and interests mostly of a material sort, knowing nothing of the world of science and philosophy, art and literature. The great drama of history is a blank to him. He is not inspired by its lessons, its noble characters and stirring events. He knows nothing of the marvels of literature—Homer, Æschylus, the Hebrew prophets, Dante, Shakespeare, Goethe—nothing of architecture, sculpture, painting, or music, nothing of the great discoveries and inventions that cast all the fairy tales into the shadow, and suggest a world of boundless possibilities. Again, he knows nothing of his own nature, origin, or destiny, except, perhaps, certain childish myths that grew up before science was born. The great truths of ethics, politics, economics, philosophy are beyond his ken, so that he hardly knows what the words mean. Thus, on all sides, he is hampered, fettered, shut up in a bare, squalid, narrow world, dark within and dark without. In such a world he has small opportunity for freedom. He is thankful, if he can walk in some beaten track and keep out of mischief. And, indeed, he often fails to do even that. He is, moreover, forced to confine himself to dull, ignorant, perhaps coarse company, and to such low forms of enjoyment as smoking, drinking, gambling, roughness, or even worse vices. And, indeed, what else should we expect from a man shut up by ignorance and unculture in a dull, monotonous Devil's Island prison? Of all the sad effects of ignorance, perhaps the saddest is, that it cuts its victims off from the society of intelligent and cultured men and women. It is utterly vain to try to make the cultured and the uncultured man meet socially on common ground. With the best of wills they cannot do it. . . . Thus the ignorant are condemned to associate with the ignorant, and to be cut off from the world of intelligence and culture—from the very influences which they most need. But this is surely a lamentable state of affairs, especially in a democratic country, where intelligent citizenship is demanded of everybody. Are we not, as a nation, unfaithful to our own principles, if we allow it to continue? Are we not endangering the very existence of our free institutions? Are we not, as individuals, guilty of heartless cruelty to our brothers and sisters, in allowing them to be disinherited of their share in the great treasures of spiritual goods heaped up by the labors of past generations? How can any learned and cultured man or woman look his or her ignorant and neglected brother or sister in the face and not blush with shame?

The practical question is, How shall an end be put to this utterly disgraceful condition of things? In other words, the chief educational problem which the nineteenth century passes on to the twentieth is, By what means shall every citizen in the nation receive such a training for body and soul as shall enable him to enjoy all the treasures of culture won by past generations, and to take part in all the activities of life with intelligence, energy, and beneficence? There are other problems, but they are subordinate to this.

It is surely clear that the institutions needed in a democracy are such as shall wipe out all the unbrothering distinctions that divide sect from sect, and shall use every effort to secure for the whole body of the people intellectual, moral, political, and economic freedom.

It appears, then, that the People's or Breadwinners University which our circumstances demand must consist of two parts: (1) a College for Culture; and (2) a Polytechnic Institute for Professional Training. Let us consider the nature of (a) the Culture; and (b) the Training which these must, respectively, give in order to be truly efficient.

a. *Culture*

Culture, it is obvious, must extend to the whole human being, body and soul, and to all their functions. It should never be forgotten that it is difference of culture, far more than difference of wealth or position, that separates man from man and class from class.

Body culture includes health, strength, grace, and dexterity, which are acquired, respectively, through hygienics, gymnastics, deportment, and manual training. The whole of these should be taught in the lower schools; but they must be continued in the Breadwinners University—the first three in the College, the last in the Polytechneum. In the department of Hygienics pupils will be taught what to eat and drink, how to prepare it, and when and in what quantities to take it. They will be taught when and how to sleep and how to avoid all those excesses which weaken and break down the nervous system. They will be taught how to avoid the evils of unsanitary homes and unsanitary dressing. No one who has not looked into the matter knows how much the working classes suffer from lack of knowledge of the laws of hygiene. Ill-fed, ill-clad, accustomed to breathe impure air, they are unable to do their best work, and are wont to be sour and ill-tempered. Look at many of the young people in the streets and note what complexions they have. That means bad food, bad digestion, bad air, bad care. It may be said that good food costs too much; but that is only half true. There are many inexpensive foods that are excellent; and even dear food is often the cheapest in the long run. All this will be explained in the class in Hygienics. In the class in Gymnastics every exercise will be taught that can impart strength and suppleness to the body, and make it the ready instrument of the soul. The practice of Gymnastics should be continued throughout the entire life, in order to insure readiness of action. What is more unbecoming than high or stooping shoulders, a sideling or rolling gait, a slow, ungainly movement of hands and feet, a general looseness and feebleness of the whole frame? And these things are not only unbecoming, but they also go far to unfit their victims for skilled labor and efficient work. Gymnastics, it should be remembered, are a great aid to hygiene, if they do not degenerate into athletics, which are often extremely unhygienic, not to say brutalizing. In the class in Deportment everything will be done to train the body in ease, dignity, and grace, and impart refinement of manners. It is, to a large extent, the lack of these that unfits the uncultivated man for mingling with cultivated people. In their society he feels awkward and bashful. He feels that everybody is looking at him. He does not know how to act at table, in a drawing-room, in a public assembly, and so on. The man of boorish manners, who talks loud, uses slang, puts his elbows on the table, and eats with his knife, cannot expect to be a welcome guest among refined people. These, no doubt, seem little things and they are; but they are big enough to separate class from class, which is not a little thing. There is no reason in the world why men and women who have to earn their living by manual labor should not be as refined in manners and bearing as any other class of the people. It is, largely, the lack of this refinement that makes so many of them willing to live in squalor and that makes the other classes look down upon them as inferiors, and their employers treat them as mere "hands."

Soul culture must extend to all the three faculties or aspects of the soul—the intellect, the affections, and the will—and be such as to develop these harmoniously to their full extent. Our present schools and universities do little more than attempt to train the first of these, leaving the other two to take care of themselves. The result is that the affections and wills even of those few who receive a university education remain in the condition of mere caprice, undisciplined and misdirected. In the Breadwinners University not only the intellect, but also the affections and the will must be educated and trained. Let us consider these faculties in this order.

1. The Intellect. What sort of education shall the intellect of the breadwinner receive? In attempting to answer this question, I am assuming that all those who desire higher education have already acquired the lower branches which the state socialistically provides in the common schools; that they can read, write, and cipher; that they know something of geography, physical and political, grammar, physical science, music, drawing, etc. What higher studies shall they undertake? The answer seems obvious: those studies which shall show them their place in the great drama of nature and history and the part they have to play in it. This is what we mean by imparting culture. The man who knows what he is, whence he is, whither he is going, how he is related to the world and his fellows, is the cultured man. He may not know Sanskrit or Arabic, or even Greek and Latin; he may know very little of chemistry, botany, or astronomy, and nothing of quaternions; yet he will have the essential things. All the studies I have named are important, but they are not essential to culture. Now what are the sciences that teach us our place and part in the world? They may all be included under one—the science of evolution. Our place in the world is our place in the process of evolution. What we are consists of what we have done and what we are going to do. But the sciences of what we have done and are going to do are two—history and sociology—the former supplying the facts, and the latter the theory of the facts. History includes not merely the evolution of humanity, but the whole course of evolution—the story of the world; and sociology, which is the true philosophy, shows the principles by which this evolution is guided, thus enabling us individually to play our part in it. The facts of history may be classed under various heads, such as natural and cultural; and these again may be subdivided, the former into astronomical, chemical, geological, biological, psychological, etc.; the latter into religious, ethical, political, economic, aesthetic, etc. But all these divisons are made merely for convenience of treatment, and the science of sociology shows that they are all but aspects of one eternal process, in which each of us has an eternal part to play.

I know nothing more inspiring than the world view to which a true and exhaustive sociology leads. It is, in truth, religion made scientific; for what else has religion ever been but a view of man's relations to the society of beings that form his environment and of his duties in these relations? In these days when, in the pitiless glare of scientific research, the old unscientific world views which formed the basis of earlier religions are passing away, it is of utmost importance that they should be replaced by a scientific one. Unless this is done, religion, which lends to life all the sublimity and consecration it has, must disappear, and life become vulgar, sordid, selfish, and frivolous, as, indeed, it is obviously becoming at present, just for want of such a world view. Kant once said: "Two things move me to ever greater awe: the starry heaven above and the moral law within." There is one thing more awe-inspiring than either of these, one thing that includes them both and much more—the spectacle of the process of the world through beginningless, endless years, a process which embraces the starry heavens and the moral heavens alike. History, in its full and original sense (*ἱστορία*), is the record of all this, of the gradual ascent from matter to mind, from sense and desire to intelligence and love and will. And the record must be complete if we are to understand ourselves and guide our lives aright. We must first know our relations to the subhuman world, to minerals, plants, and animals of all grades; for, indeed, we are related to them all, and are cousins to birds, serpents, fishes, and apes; then our relations to the starry heavens, and finally our relations to our fellow human beings. We must follow the gradual progress of man up from the earliest dawn of intelligence; from the lowest savage condition, when he knew not the use of fire or weapons, up through the stone age, the bronze age, the iron age. We must follow the growth of primitive societies, at first small and weak, on to ever larger combinations—villages, towns, cities, kingdoms, empires. We must study the histories of Chaldea, Assyria, Babylonia, Egypt, Media, Persia, of the Hebrews, Greeks, Romans, and all the rest, down to our own day. Then we shall see that it is all one great drama, in which the histories of those different peoples are but so many acts or scenes. And what a drama it is, with its heroes and saints, its martyrs and conquerors, its merchants and statesmen, its poets and sages, its prophets and messiahs! What interest arises as we watch and comprehend it!

And we are the outcome of all this. We each bear in our bodies and souls the result of the entire process. We are the sum of the whole Past; the whole Past is needed to explain us; and, for that matter, the whole future also. We were born yesterday, so to speak; but our history goes back to the beginning of things. I cannot fully answer the question, What am I? without knowing the whole of History and Sociology. I cannot understand or properly appreciate the government of the United States, that flower of the ages, except on the same condition. Why are we so devoted to freedom, and why do we look down upon nations like Russia and Turkey that are not free? History and Sociology alone can tell us. And how inspiring Sociology is! How instructive it is to follow the phases of religion, ethics, economics, politics, etc., from the dawn of culture to our own day! How interesting each new discovery in archaeology, in language, in mythology, becomes to us! In the light of such study how plain the meaning of the movements of the present day is—of socialism, anarchism, and the rest! Were it not that History and Sociology are badly taught in our schools and colleges, taught in a fragmentary, unsystematic, and ungenetic way, these movements would be seen to be mere reversions to primitive conditions. It is quite usual to begin the study of History with the History of the United States, and of Sociology with the works of Herbert Spencer. As well might we begin the study of Mathematics with the differential calculus, or Manual Training with the construction of a steam engine! In the Breadwinners Colleges of the future these sciences must be taught so as to reveal the whole process of evolution in which alone the different phases are intelligible.

To draw up a course of study for a Breadwinners College is not easy; but the following may be regarded as a first attempt.

1. Outline of the Course of Evolution, including Philosophy of Evolution
2. The Circle of the Sciences (Encyclopaedie), including Doctrine of Method
3. Outlines of Universal History and Sociology
4. Comparative Religion, including Philosophy of Religion
5. Comparative Ethics, including Philosophy of Ethics
6. Comparative Politics, including Political Philosophy
7. Comparative Literature, including Theory of Criticism
8. Comparative Art, including Philosophy of Æsthetics
9. History and Philosophy of Economics
10. History of Discoveries and Inventions, and Influence of these
11. History and Philosophy of Education
12. Comparative Philology, including Philosophy of Language
13. History of Philosophy and Philosophic Concepts
14. Outlines of Psychology, including History of Psychological Theories

It is obvious, I think, that any person pursuing such a curriculum as this would, at the end, have a fair conception of the process of the world he lives in and of his own place in it. He would, moreover, have his horizon greatly widened, his interests multiplied and deepened, and his life lifted above the narrow, sordid cares of the present. He would no longer be the victim of every social and political quack who had a nostrum to advertise. But, of course, it will said that such a curriculum is far beyond the intellectual reach of the great body of wage-earners. To this I can only reply that, in my belief, based upon a pretty intimate acquaintance with the working classes, it is a profound mistake. Everything depends upon how knowledge is presented. If the above curriculum were presented in dry academic lectures, I admit that it could not be followed by many of the breadwinners; but that is the poorest way of presenting knowledge, and there is no necessity for so presenting it. As Froebel is never tired of telling us, all true education comes through self-activity. The teacher who does least himself, and makes his pupils do most, is the best teacher. Let an instructor take any one of the above subjects, say the first, and let him, after a brief, simple, introductory talk, divide it into topics, or subjects for essays, assigning one of these to each of his pupils, and telling him where—in what books or museums—the necessary information may be found. Then, at future meetings, let the pupils read their essays, carefully corrected by the instructor, before the class, and the class freely discuss them, and it will be found that there is no lack of ability or interest among the breadwinners. If the instructor have time—and why should he not?—he will do well to accompany his pupils to museums and galleries, and on excursions into city and country, that they may make acquaintance with facts and nature face to face.

The first essays of the breadwinners attempting to write on scientific subjects will, no doubt, in most cases, be crude and styleless, and their reading indistinct and hesitating; but these defects will soon pass away, and the sons of toil will have learned to write and read, in addition to the science acquired. What is more, they will have learned to take interest in books, in nature, and in social conditions.

The above curriculum, which would extend over three or four years, might be interspersed with other studies in particular departments of literature and science, care being taken that these entered into integral relations with the whole and contributed to a single world-view. Their place in the "Circle of the Sciences" should be clearly marked.

So much for the culture of the intellect.

2. *The Affections.* How shall the affections of the breadwinners be elicited in such a way that they shall distribute their intensity in proportion to the true,

spiritual worth of things? That is the all-important question; for, as the ancients and Dante saw clearly, all moral evil arises from a false distribution of the affections, all moral worth from a true distribution of them. The fact is, the affections or desires are the most fundamental part of us, more primitive than intellect and will; and so long as they are not right, nothing is right. "Out of the heart are the issues of life."

It is a well-known law that every faculty is developed through its proper object or "good"—sight by things visible, intelligence by things knowable, will by things doable, and so on. It follows that the affections are developed by things desirable or lovable, and that, if they are to be properly developed, things must be adhered to or appreciated by them in the order of their desirability, that is, their worth for moral life. The question is, How can this be accomplished? Nobility is more desirable than wealth: how can this be brought home to the affections? This is a very different question from, How can an intellectual apprehension or conviction of this be imparted? Intellectual convictions are feeble motives to action, compared with affections. A man who loves nobility will be far more noble than the man who knows that nobility is lovable. How then shall we make people love nobility more than wealth? The answer is, By presenting each in its complete reality. This may be done in various ways—in the home, in the school, in the course of practical life—but the most effective way is through art, whose function it is to present things in such a way as to reveal their true meaning or moral worth. Dante's *Hell* and *Purgatory,* by showing the true nature of sin, make it very unlovable, while his *Paradise,* by showing the true nature of righteousness, makes it most desirable. How we hate hypocrisy after reading *Measure for Measure;* reckless ambition, after reading *Macbeth;* indecision, after reading *Hamlet,* and so on! Who can intelligently look at the Laocoön group without hating sensual vice; or at the Praxitelean Hermes without loving the spiritual sympathy that longs to educate?

The modern world has rarely realized the function of art, and hence an infinite amount of nonsense and sentimental twaddle has been spoken and written about it; but the ancients, especially the Greeks, were not so blind. Aristotle saw clearly that art addresses itself to the affections . . . and is calculated to effect their purification, that is, to free them from disorder, obtuseness, and exaggeration. His notions regarding the place of music in education are only now beginning to be appreciated.

As science is only distilled intellectual experience, so the fine arts are only distilled emotional or affectional experience. And just as there is, at the present day, a movement to limit book-science, and to accord a considerable space in intellectual education to direct contact with nature, so the affectional culture derivable from the fine arts should be supplemented by emotional training through direct contact with the life of man. The students in the Breadwinners Colleges, while emotionally realizing the works of Homer, Dante, Shakespeare, Goethe, Phidias, Praxiteles, da Vinci, and the rest of the mighty, should be using the emotional culture thus gained to penetrate the life about them, its joys and sorrows, its loves and aspirations, and thus to enter into sympathetic, that is normal, relations with their fellow-men. And no one will have more ample opportunities for this than just these students. More than almost any one, they are brought face to face with "life's prime needs and agonies," and thus have a chance for a better education than any one else. There is nothing that is more truly educative, nothing that better insures a correct distribution of the affections, than philanthropic work of the right sort, undertaken, not in a spirit of condescension or missionariness, but in simple loving-kindness, and reduced to a habit. The last clause deserves to be emphasized; for it should never be forgotten that in the training of the affections habit plays a very important part. We love what we are familiar with, and what we can do easily.

3. The Will. When the body is strong and healthy,

when the intelligence is carefully trained through study and contact with nature, and when the affections are distributed in accordance with the true worth of things, then there will be little need to worry over the training of the will. The will, indeed, is little more than the combined expression of the rational and irrational elements in the soul, in other words, the sum of the irrational impulses directed by rational insight. The breadwinner is a privileged being as far as will training is concerned; for his daily labor calls for almost continual exertion of will. If in the Breadwinners Colleges there is to be a will trainer, his chief function will be to select and assign tasks suited to the intellectual and affectional status of his different pupils. Such tasks will be the more effective in proportion to the amount of patience and self-denial they call for; that is, in proportion as they induce the individual to prefer his all-inclusive, to his all-exclusive, self, and to sacrifice his fragmentary self of the moment to the fully organized self of his entire existence. To live for all men and for eternity is to live a divine life, here and now.

So much for Culture and Culture Colleges. There is nothing in the smallest degree impractical in the scheme of Breadwinners Colleges here proposed. Indeed, we see it in process of realization in France at the present moment. The infamy accruing to that country from the "Dreyfus case" roused three different classes of her people—Wealth, Wisdom, and Work—to ask themselves this question: What must be the intellectual and moral condition of a nation in which such things can be done and brave publicity. And realizing at once its abjectness and danger, they united in an attempt to put an end to it by diffusing intellectual and moral culture among the great body of the people, that previously had been left in ignorance, or to the tender mercies of the daily newspaper and the priest. Thus have come into existence in a very brief space of time a large number of so-called "Popular Universities" . . . What the French have done we certainly can do, and ought to do. If their intellectual and moral condition is fraught with peril, ours is certainly not encouraging. Let us think but a moment of the condition of our chief city, governed by a ring of vulgar adventurers, whose sole aim, by their own confession, is to fill their own pockets; who protect and encourage the coarsest vices that they may fatten on the blackmail levied on their perpetrators; who bribe and are bribed; for whom evil is good and good is evil! Where such things can boldly flaunt themselves, there is surely need for popular education. Realizing our disgraceful condition, our better men and women, from time to time, work themselves up into virtuous fury, and demand legislation and other external contrivances to put a stop to it, never realizing that it is impossible to obtain any better condition until the people are better, and that they will not be better until they are better educated. They try everything but the one thing that has any prospect of being effectual. As the people are, so are their rulers. And what sort of rulers are people likely to choose, a large number of whom live in squalor and poverty, condemned to a mean, beggarly world, occupied with sordid material interests, unillumined by science, art, philosophy, or history? We have but to look and see. Surely, then, it is time for the three classes of the people to unite to found Breadwinners Colleges.

b. *Professional Training*

Thus far I have spoken of Culture, which opens up to the worker a noble world, invites him to come in, and renders him capable in body and soul of enjoying it and mingling with the best. It is the glory of our nation that no door leading to anything desirable is closed against the man of culture, be he Jew or Gentile, rich or poor. But on this earth of ours we need not only culture in order to live a normal human life, but also the means of living. We need the former in order to live well, the latter in order to live at all. The higher laws and needs of our being do not abrogate the lower; they come not to destroy but to fulfill. Culture will make good men and women, good sons and daughters, good husbands and wives, good fathers and mothers, good neighbors and citizens, and so on; but it does not make good mechanics, merchants, bankers, physicians, lawyers, teachers, or artists. For these and many other professions, none of which are essential to us as human beings or citizens, there is needed a special training. Much of this may be, and is, imparted in the actual practice of the different industries; but there is much that cannot be so imparted, and demands special institutions.

. . . .

3. *The higher education in this country is not given under such circumstances that all can take advantage of it.* Nearly all of its institutions—colleges, universities, polytechnic institutes, technical and industrial schools—are closed against the breadwinners, because they are occupied with their work during the day, the only time when these institutions are open. *What the breadwinners need is evening colleges and evening polytechneums.* The feasibility of evening colleges may be seen in the work of the London Polytechnic, of the London Working Men's College, and of many similar institutions in Great Britain—"Mechanics' Institutes" and the like. That evening polytechneums are equally within the limits of possibility, and may even be a great success, is shown by the fact that they are a success in London and elsewhere. It is needless to dwell at great length on this subject, the facts of it, and the way out are so evident. They were known even to Luther, who says: "My opinion is that we must send boys to school one or two hours a day, and have them learn a trade at home the rest of the time. It is desirable that these two occupations go side by side." At present it is clear that the "one or two hours" must be in the evening.

Such are a few suggestions toward a solution of the chief educational problem which the nineteenth century hands over to the twentieth. There is little time left for the consideration of minor problems, such as the training of efficient teachers for all grades of education; the arrangements and coordination of studies in view of different ends; the unifying of the whole course of study from the kindergarten up to the university; the establishment of a National University to give tone and direction to the whole national system of education, etc.

The one problem which above all others cries aloud for solution, and which it will be one of the chief tasks of the twentieth century to solve, is the higher education of the breadwinners. This education is absolutely necessary not only for the well being of the breadwinners themselves, but for the safety of our whole nation and its democratic institutions. A democracy cannot long be sustained by an ignorant demos. This, indeed, is already becoming manifest. Our labor unions have already interfered with the liberty not only of employers and of the public generally, but also, and still more, of the individual workman. Tyranny, socialism, and violent anarchism, with their glittering utopias, are finding adherents among the workingmen. The political boss, with his lying promises and his filthy bribes, finds many of them as easy prey. All these things are fraught with serious dangers to liberty, and they are all due to want of intellectual and moral education. On the other hand, it is to the want of technical training that is due the fact that a very large number of our people are unable by their labor to give to society an equivalent for a decent livelihood, and therefore live in poverty and squalor, which are always powerful incentives to vice, crime, and rebellion. To the lack of the two kinds of education combined is due, in a word, all that we deplore and all that we fear in the condition of the breadwinners.

And for this condition we are all responsible. We leave a large number of them without intellectual and moral culture, and then we despise them because they are ignorant and vicious. We do nothing to refine their manners, and then we complain because they are boorish or brutal. We do not train them in the principles of political economy or sociology, and then we wonder why they become socialists, anarchists, or nihilists. We leave them unacquainted with their political privileges and duties, and then we are indignant because they sell their votes for a glass of whisky. We consign them to dark, cheerless, comfortless homes and then we berate them because they take refuge in the gilded saloon. We give them no opportunity for the spiritual delights that come from the arts and sciences, and then we scorn them because they seek satisfaction in rum drinking and the other sensual delights of the dive. To offset the saloon, the dive, and the pool room, we open quiet reading-rooms and chaperoned recreation-rooms, and we wonder that they are not attractive to people who have never learned to take delight in reading or in quiet recreation. All these failures and wonderments on our part leave them in a deplorable condition, and build up between us and them a wall of alienation and misunderstanding that not only suggests a "war of classes" in the future, but is narrowing and blinding to both classes now. The rich and the learned are poorer and meaner because they cannot enter into brotherly and sisterly relations with the toilers; and these suffer equally because they are sundered from those. Nothing can bring about that sympathy of classes which is so essential to a democracy and so beneficial to all classes but the universal diffusion of culture. The true rivals to the saloon, the dive, and the pool-room are the Breadwinners College and Polytechneum, with their lectures, their classes, their exhibitions, and their practical work.

There is money enough and talent enough in this city of New York to give a higher education to all the people if they would but demand it. If but half the money that is spent in preaching old fables, and obsolete, semi-barbarous moralities were devoted to the truly religious purpose of developing the bodies and enlightening the souls of them that sit in darkness, we should soon have a different world about us. To-day we need something very different from, and more effective than, the weekly sermon and the catechism. And, above all, we need to learn that the simple doing of our duty in all the relations of life is the only worthy religion. In that religion there are no sects; there is neither Jew nor Gentile.

Let us all hope that ere the twentieth century reaches its majority there will be in every city ward and in every country township a People's University, consisting of a College for physical, intellectual, and moral culture and a Polytechneum for professional training. So only will it be well with us and our country.

11

University Education for Those Unable to Attend a University

AMERICAN SOCIETY FOR THE EXTENSION OF UNIVERSITY TEACHING

The acclimatization of ideas and institutions imported from abroad has been one of the fairly constant enterprises of Americans from their earliest days. One can either emphasize the origin of the ideas and institutions, thus establishing cultural continuities with Europe, or their adaption, thus emphasizing their Americanization. The history of university extension in the United States is a history of institutional borrowing (from England), acclimatization, and elaboration of the acclimated idea. Herbert Baxter Adams (1850-1901), the historian, the pioneer propagandist for university extension in the United States, tried at first to find lodgment for the idea in the public libraries. This did not work. In 1890 the American Society for the Extension of University Teaching, of Philadelphia, undertook to acclimatize the English idea by establishing an independent organization to manage the service, but drawing upon the universities for teachers. In spite of the very high quality of the teachers who cooperated in the work with adults—James Breasted, E. G. Conklin, F. H. Giddings, J. B. McMaster, J. H. Robinson, H. J. Mackinder, Graham Wallas, Hilaire Belloc, and others—this effort also failed, but only after twenty-six years of existence (1890-1916). However, from 1890 to 1900 the ASEUT flourished to a very promising degree. The following document, drawn from Ten Years Report of the American Society for the Extension of University Teaching, 1890-1900 *(Philadelphia, 1901), gives the gist of the ASEUT's rationale. It still exudes the idealism which originally inspired the effort to bring higher education to the man-on-the-street. In the same decade that the ASEUT was most vigorously flourishing, universities, mostly in the Middle West, began to experiment with the idea as a wholly university enterprise. After much further work at acclimatization, the most decisive of which was done at Wisconsin, a truly American university extension was evolved and, about 1910, began to assume its present highly elaborate shape.*

In 1878, Sidney Lanier, writing on the subject of lecturing said: "During my studies for the last six or eight months, a thought which was at first vague, has slowly crystalized into a purpose of quite decisive aim. The lectures which I was invited to deliver last winter before a private class, met with such an enthusiastic reception as to set me thinking very seriously of the evident delight with which grown people found themselves receiving systematic instruction in a definite study. The fault of the lecture system as at present conducted—a fault which must finally prove fatal to it—is that it is too fragmentary, and presents too fragmentary a mass of facts before the hearers. Now if a scheme of lectures should be arranged which would amount to the systematic presentation of a given subject, then the audience would receive substantial benefit, and would carry away some genuine possession at the end of the course. This stage of the investigation put me to thinking of schools for grown people. Men and women leave college nowadays just at the time when they are really prepared to study with effect."

The thought of Sidney Lanier had already found expression in England through the plans and activities of the Cambridge and London Societies for the Extension of University Teaching. They were founded respectively in 1873 and 1876. Similar work was begun by the University of Oxford in 1878, and made effective in 1885 through the impulse given by the hand of Mr. Michael E. Sadler.

In 1890 Professor Richard G. Moulton came to Philadelphia, informed as to all that had been done in England and inspired by a consciousness of the potential force contained in the new educational idea. The response to the appeal contained in his lectures was prompt and generous. The American Society was founded, with Dr. William Pepper as its first President. Many of those who to-day are firm supporters of the Society were among its first members; there are many who, from the beginning until now, have never failed in loyalty or in direct assistance when their aid was needed. Mr. Frederick B. Miles has served uninterruptedly in the office of Treasurer. The aim of University Extension as then officially stated by the English Societies was this: "To attempt to solve the problem of how much of what the Universities do for their own students can be done for people unable to go to the Universities."

This idea is a noble one, and it awakened the enthusiasm that looks for great and immediate results as well as that which nerves to prolonged and steady effort. There came a time when zeal of the first sort flagged a little, but there was enough of the staying kind to sustain, until results that were necessarily slow of growth began at last to be apparent.

To instruct people who are not obliged to go to school, it is necessary to awaken a desire to learn. To do this was a large part of the Society's work in its early years. It had to send out its missionaries and interest before it taught. The mission work was well done; the idea of University Extension found lodgment in all parts of the country. In some places it has had a permanent and important influence; in others it has shown no real vitality. Nothing comes out of University Extension unless a great deal is put into it; the desire to give, of the best, should be always somewhat more intense than the wish to receive.

As aids, in bringing its purposes before people, the Society published a magazine called *University Extension,* and a paper, *The Bulletin.* They were widely distributed and at first they were doubtless read; but the time came when themes connected with University Extension had lost their freshness, or the initial interest in a new subject had waned. At all events these journals were no longer read. Then an attempt was made to have a paper of more general interest—one that would supplement the Society's teaching by lecturers. *The Citizen* was launched in 1895. It seemed to have the respect of persons whose good opinion was valuable, when they were brought to read it, but its prestige was not sufficient for its purpose; we lacked the resources to conduct the paper as a commercial enterprise, and it made no headway in competition with magazines that must be made to pay, and therefore made attractive to the casual reader. Since August 1898, the Society has had no periodical publication.

There have been published, however, from the beginning, the syllabi of the lecture courses. The syllabi are constantly improving in respect to fullness, and care in preparation. They now form a large collection of outlines for study and reading and cover a wide field.

In a review of the Society's work, mention should be made of the Summer Meetings. Five have been held—in the years 1893-1897. Their purpose was to afford special opportunities for close and continuous study on the part of University Extension students, and teachers; to bring together the people of the various Centres and to stimulate the desire for the best that University Extension had to offer.

In England, for many years, such meetings have been held with success at Oxford and Cambridge, under the auspices of those great Universities, and with the use of their grounds and buildings. The Summer School of Harvard University is an instance in this country of somewhat similar work well done. The University of Pennsylvania liberally put at the disposition of the Society accommodations for its meetings, and for five years these gatherings took place in July.

Here again the serious purposes of the Society interfered possibly with an apparent success. There was little or no provision for those who wanted entertainment rather than teaching; and we know that the thirst for learning must be strong to induce people to study hard in Philadelphia for four weeks in July.

There was an average of 175 students at these meetings. The average yearly cost was $3,273.79; sixty-one per cent being paid by the students. The yearly deficit to be met by the Society was between $1,200 and $1,300.

The amount of labor and the expense entailed by the Summer Meetings were quite out of proportion to the physical powers of the Society's staff and to the money at command. It was found that the meetings were not so much for our own students as for strangers from a distance who did not know Philadelphia in July. There have been no Summer Meetings since 1897. They were undertaken in sincerity and worked at with devotion until it seemed evident that the effort and money expended could be better applied to the distinctive work of the Society, leaving summer schools for cooler places. Nevertheless the Summer Meetings brought to Philadelphia, as students and teachers, many influential persons who went away with a respect for University Extension that they had perhaps refused to it, as seen from farther off.

It will be remembered that the University Lecture Association, beginning in 1887, gave for a few years a large number of afternoon lectures. When the Association was dissolved, in 1895, your Society undertook to have each season two afternoon courses, carrying out the plan of the Association, although modified by making the number of courses fewer and of a character to command attention. This plan has worked well. These are the only lectures given directly by the General Society instead of through the action of its local Centres. The lectures of one of these courses, given in Philadelphia in the winter of 1898-99, have been published by Houghton Mifflin Company, in a volume entitled *Counsel upon the Reading of Books.*

No aspect of the life of your Society is more significant and gratifying than the relation to it of its Centres and the co-operation of those who manage the local bodies. Unpaid, often at the expense of their own pockets, upwards of five thousand people have joined in our efforts, working hard with their neighbors, to arrange for lecture courses; to find meeting places; to sell tickets; to pay deficits; and persevering, until the demand created gathered strength enough to make good Centres.

Sometimes the General Society has been able to help Centres over hard places by a special lecture or by aid in money. On the other hand Centres that have prospered, and sometimes those that have known trouble, have contributed liberally to the General Society.

In New Jersey the Centres have an association. Their representatives meet yearly for consultation and discussion. Occasionally there are meetings of a more general character including delegates from all the Centres within reach of Philadelphia.

As the Society has grown older we have come to know better its field and its purposes. Nothing haunts the laborer in our vineyard more persistently than the question: "Does University Extension reach the people it was intended for?" We should like to believe that our answer will be final, but we know better.

University Extension is meant for those for whom religion is intended; for those for whom life, liberty, and the pursuit of happiness is intended. It is meant to help the ignorant who desire knowledge—that they may learn wisely; to reveal to the half educated the insufficiency of their knowledge; to arouse intellectual sluggards; to stimulate those who are in the right way; to bring questioning to the hearts of the self-satisfied. There is no class for which University Extension is not intended nor to which it has not ministered. There have been courses, not a few but many, to audiences made up entirely of the very poor; of the poor; of the poor and of those who are not rich; of these and of the well-to-do; of the ignorant but eager; of the cultivated but not learned; of teachers; we might almost say—having in mind the Summer Meetings—of scholars: finally, of people of all conditions who have some leisure for study or reading and look to your lecturers for suggestions and leading.

If the University Extension is intended for so many, the number of those who have profited by it should be great. We find this to be so. The average number of people each year who have attended our courses is a little more than 18,000. The total course attendance for ten years amounts to 180,755, which is equivalent to an aggregate attendance of 1,084,530. The attendance has been larger in the last two years than at any previous time. In these years there has been an average attendance of 243 people for each lecture. There were given in the two years 1,056 lectures. Last year the average attendance at the classes after the lectures was 149, or sixty-two per cent of the audiences. These results were accomplished at an expense to the General Society in 1900 of a little more than $6,000.

If it is assumed that the teaching was better than the average of University teaching—and this may be maintained—it can be said that your Society is a People's University, teaching where it is convenient for the people to get together, in hours not given to labor. The teaching is often intermittent and sometimes discursive. It is addressed to the many and it can not always meet special needs, but it is earnest, systematic, and painstaking. It must interest or it can not be given. What the sum of the influences is it is hard to say, but considering the maturity and the numbers of those who listen, who read as a consequence, and to reading add thinking, the influence is likely rather to be underestimated than appraised too highly.

In looking back over ten years we find two results of experience that are worth mention. First, it is found that the best results are attained in Centres that have a sustained activity; that attempt to have some relation between the courses given, and incline rather to intensive than to discursive study. The results are educationally better, and it is easier to pay expenses in these Centres than in those demanding too much variety. Secondly, it is all important that lecturers should be up to the work —in knowledge of their subjects; in enthusiasm for teaching; in the care taken in preparation; in the gift of presentation, and in personal character.

Few things are more difficult to do effectively than University Extension teaching; it is hard enough to do it well when it is made a vocation: the men are few who can succeed, taking it up as an avocation. One of the greatest difficulties your directors have met is in finding competent men. The number of those who are willing to try is unlimited; those who can reasonably be expected to do well, and are willing to put their hearts and souls into the work, are few, and hard to find. How far we have succeeded in this direction we must leave to your judgment, referring you to the list of lecturers. We think, however, that as the difficulties of our task have become more apparent there has been a corresponding effort to overcome them; that with higher ideals concerning the way the work should be done it has been better done; that it has gained rather than lost ground in the estimation of the community and of educators.

The total cost of the Society's work for ten years has been $275,000: of this $183,000 has been earned and $92,000 has been given. There have been over five thousand lectures. The Centres have found, in addition to the $183,000 received from them by the General Society, about $55,000 for local expenses. The total expense, therefore, has been $330,000. Of this amount $238,000 has been paid by the people of the Centres; $22,000 by members of the General Society contributing $5 each, and $70,000 by guarantors and those making special contributions. The total number of contributors has been 1,722 and the average of subscriptions, above $5, has been $150 a year.

Has not the time come for the endowment of the Society, that its future may be assured, that it may have the means of assuring men competent for University Extension lecturing that they will find in it a career that is neither precarious nor unrewarded?

As for the fruits of the first ten years of your Society's work, besides the direct results already mentioned, we know of the establishment of libraries; the renewed use of libraries that had been almost forgotten; a demand for travelling libraries; the more intelligent reading of books; the use of books of the better sort; the introduction of new and vital interests, especially in small communities; improvement in the character of school teaching; higher standards for public lectures; the creation of new ideals in literature and art, and everywhere, the stimulation of individuals to better conceptions of the pleasure of life.

A well-known citizen of Philadelphia, one familiar with University Extension but not connected with its administration, recently expressed publicly the following opinion: "The American Society for the Extension of University Teaching, which has now been at work for ten years, has not only succeeded in doing more than any one agency in revolutionizing the reading habits of Philadelphia, but it has created a solid, organized group of audiences, habituated to study, anxious to learn, interested in the intellectual development not only of themselves but of the city, which constitutes a constituency and clientele such as does not exist in any other American city, and which is to-day one of the most useful agencies for promoting the solidarity of the intellectual life of Philadelphia."

If this statement is true—and, if it can be said of the work in Philadelphia, it is also true, to a considerable extent of the same influence in other places—then your Society has justified its being and has become a social force of the first importance.

12

The Sociology of the Diffusion of Knowledge

LESTER F. WARD

Lester F. Ward (1841-1913) is remembered as a peer of Comte and Spencer among the great pioneers of sociology. He developed his sociological conceptions while in the employ of the federal government as a botanist and geologist, publishing about as many books in those fields as in sociology. He became professor of sociology at Brown University only in 1906 and in the same year was chosen first president of the American Sociological Society. On the title page of Applied Sociology: a Treatise on the Conscious Improvement of Society by Society *(1906), from which the following passages were selected,* Ward quoted Adolphe Coste as saying, "L'application est la pierre de touche de toute doctrine." Adult education can be argued to be an application of Ward's doctrine of the central importance of the wide diffusion of knowledge in society's effort consciously to improve itself. This was perceived at the time by President C. R. Van Hise of the University of Wisconsin who cited Ward in support of the University's work in university extension. As a matter of fact, Ward's argumentation is, in historical perspective, a classic defense, in*

* Reprinted by permission of Ginn and Company.

sociological terms, of all adult education that involves the diffusion of knowledge.

In the administration of the social estate the first and principal task is to hunt up all the heirs and give to each his share. But every member of society is equally the heir to the entire social heritage, and, as we have already seen, all may possess it without depriving any of any part of it. And as the social heritage consists of the knowledge that has been brought into the world, this task is nothing less than the diffusion of all knowledge among all men. When this knowledge is properly classified it falls into natural groups and consists of a series of great truths. These truths contain within them a multitude of minor truths, but these minor truths need not be all actually possessed by every mind. They are really known when the general truths are known, but the extent to which they are specially appropriated may be left optional. All will select some of them, but different persons will require an acquaintance with different parts of this detailed knowledge according to their tastes and pursuits. For general guidance in life, and in order to occupy a position of social equality with all others, the great groups of knowledge only need to be possessed. This general knowledge is embraced in the six great sciences of the hierarchy, and if they are acquired in the order of nature they will be both easily and thoroughly acquired. This of course presupposes that the necessary instruments for their acquisition be first supplied. Such is an outline of the method of applied sociology. The rest is matter of detail.

Knowledge will always be increasing, and nothing can prevent this. Society does not need to concern itself with this. Its duty is to see that knowledge is assimilated. Its value to society not only increases with the number possessing it, but it increases according to some law of progression. It is difficult to formulate this law. A rough idea may be conveyed by saying that the value of knowledge relatively to the number possessing it increases in about the same ratio as does the value of a diamond relatively to its size. In general it may be said that the rate of increase grows constantly more rapid as universality is approached. Its full value can never be realized until universality is actually reached. When only a few possess it, it has little value. It may even be injurious. The inequalities engendered lead to all forms of exploitation and social misery. The differences of opinion that always arise from this source divide society into factions and cause all manner of strifes. Most of the evils of this nature are due to the ignorance of the most of mankind of truths that are known to a few. A large part of the war and bloodshed in the world is over matters that are already settled and may have been long settled, but only in the minds of a select number who have no means of placing the rest in possession of the truth which they possess. This is the duty of society, and the individuals possessing this knowledge are not to blame nor responsible for the resulting inequalities. Usually they do all they can to impart their knowledge to others, for . . . the mind is essentially altruistic, and next to the pleasure derived from the acquisition of knowledge and the discovery of truth, its greatest satisfaction is in imparting this knowledge and this truth to others. But those who possess knowledge are so few and those who are without it are so many that the influence of the former upon the latter is only that of a pebble dropped into the sea. Not only do wise men strive to teach everybody around them what they know, but they make great sacrifices of time and energy in writing books to spread their knowledge throughout the world and hand it down to future generations. Many establish institutions of learning and conduct them . . . largely from a sense of their usefulness to mankind. . . .

But both public and private educational institutions have always been and still remain chaotic. False notions prevail as to what education is and is for. The moment a step is made beyond the rudiments all object seems to be lost sight of, method is abandoned, organization is not thought of, and a vast mass of purposeless and useless rubbish is forced upon the learner. . . .

The only thing that can "develop" or "strengthen" the faculties of the mind is knowledge, and all real knowledge is science. The effect of this on the mind is to furnish it with something. It constitutes its contents, and, as we have seen, the power, value, and real character of mind depend upon its contents. Without knowledge the mind, however capable, is impotent and worthless. But there is a great mass of knowledge in the world. It does no good unless it is possessed by the mind. It is a power as soon as it is possessed by the mind. It is as useful to one mind as to another. It is the only working power in society, and the working power of society increases in proportion to the number possessing it—probably in a greater proportion. Only a few minds possess any considerable part of it. All are capable of possessing it all. The paramount duty of society, therefore, is to put that knowledge into the minds of all its members. . . .

The proposition that the lower classes of society are the intellectual equals of the upper classes will probably shock most minds. At least it will be almost unanimously rejected as altogether false. Yet I do not hesitate to maintain and defend it as an abstract proposition. But of course we must understand what is meant by intellectual equality. I have taken some pains to show that the difference in the intelligence of the two classes is immense. What I insist upon is that this difference in intelligence is not due to any difference in intellect. It is due entirely to difference in mental equipment. It is chiefly due to difference in knowledge, if we include in knowledge a familiarity with the tools of the mind and an acquired ability to utilize the products of human achievement . . . each age of the world's history stands on a platform erected by all past ages. It is true that all the members of society have the use to a certain extent of the products of past achievement, but in no other sense do those members stand on the elevated platform who do not actually possess the heritage of the past. Now, as a matter of fact, it is only what I have called the intelligent class who really possess this heritage. They of course possess it in varying degrees, but most of them possess enough of it to give them dominion over those who do not possess it.

I have shown . . . that social heredity is not a process of organic transmission, that no part of the social germ-plasm passes from one individual to another, but that all knowledge must be separately acquired by every individual. The social organization must be such as to infuse it into the members of society as fast as they are capable of receiving it. This infusion of it is social transmission, and unless it is infused it is not transmitted. The only way in which products of past achievement have been preserved has been through such a degree of social organization as is sufficient to infuse them into a certain number of the members of society. This number has always, in the historical races, been large enough to prevent their being lost, and most or all human achievement has been preserved. But it is easy to imagine this great social duty to be neglected and all human achievement lost. There are parts of the world in which this has virtually happened, and this is the way in which races degenerate.

But society has never and nowhere been so organized as to transmit the products of achievement to more than a small fraction of its members. These constitute the intelligent class. The rest are all intellectually disinherited, and while the intellectually disinherited always include and are nearly coextensive with the materially disinherited, the former is much the more serious condition. For the intellectual inheritance would bring with it the material inheritance and all the other advantages that are enjoyed by the intelligent class. Of all the problems of applied sociology that which towers above all others is the problem of the organization of society so that the heritage of the past shall be transmitted to all its members alike. Until this problem is solved there is scarcely any use in trying to solve other problems. Not only are most of them otherwise incapable of solution, but this primary problem once solved all others will solve themselves.

13

A Rationale of Vocational Education

COMMISSION ON NATIONAL AID TO VOCATIONAL EDUCATION

Vocational education has a long and intricate history in the United States especially if apprenticeship is included, as it should be. It was not until the 1870s, however, that the pedagogical problems of teaching vocations under classroom conditions began to be solved and not until 1914-1917 that ample funds were put behind vocational training. Funds came, from then on, from the federal government, first under the Smith-Lever Act of 1914, which established agricultural extension, and then under the Smith-Hughes Act of 1917, which made training in the industrial arts a matter of federal concern. Before that time vocational training was in the care of private enterprisers and the states. Under the impetus thus given, vocational training for adults grew like the proverbial weed and became in a short time the principal constituent of adult education. The liberal studies have never yet had the good luck to be given comparably lavish support. The text that follows is the "Summary" of The Report of the Commission on National Aid to Vocational Education, *printed in House Document 1004, 63d Congress, 2d Session. It is in effect a basic rationale for the cultivation of vocational education, and of its management, formulated in 1914, but obviously carrying a heavy freight of ideas that have been influential ever since. In our day the adequacy of this rationale is being questioned, for it is alleged not to allow for the fullest development of the individual. It is argued now that vocational education must, to justify itself, take on a new dimension and add to the equipment of even the most vocationally minded students some knowledge of the liberal studies. The document quoted below, however, is a classic formulation of a position which must be clearly understood even by the most fervent advocate of change.*

While many different kinds and grades of vocational education will always be required, the kind most urgently demanded at the present time is that which will prepare workers for the more common occupations in which the great mass of our people find useful employment.

There is a great and crying need of providing vocational education of this character for every part of the United States—to conserve and develop our resources; to promote a more productive and prosperous agriculture; to prevent the waste of human labor; to supplement apprenticeship; to increase the wage-earning power of our productive workers; to meet the increasing demand for trained workmen; to offset the increased cost of living. Vocational education is therefore needed as a wise business investment for this Nation, because our national prosperity and happiness are at stake and our position in the markets of the world can not otherwise be maintained.

The social and educational need for vocational training is equally urgent. Widespread vocational training will democratize the education of the country: (1) By recognizing different tastes and abilities and by giving an equal opportunity to all to prepare for their life work; (2) by extending education through part-time and evening instruction to those who are at work in the shop or on the farm. Vocational training will indirectly but positively affect the aims and methods of general education: (1) By developing a better teaching process through which the children who do not respond to book instruction alone may be reached and educated through learning by doing; (2) by introducing into our educational system the aim of utility, to take its place in dignity by the side of culture and to connect education with life by making it purposeful and useful. Industrial and social unrest is due in large measure to a lack of a system of practical education fitting workers for the callings. Higher standards of living are a direct result of the better education which makes workers more efficient, thus increasing their wage-earning capacity.

An overwhelming public sentiment shows the need for vocational education in this country. The testimony in this behalf comes from every class of citizenship, from the educator, the manufacturer, the trades-unionist, the business man, the social worker, and the philanthropist. Every State superintendent of public instruction declared that its rapid extension was required for many different reasons in his State and great national educational, civic, industrial, and commercial organizations, representing more than 12,000,000 people, have repeatedly gone on record as believing that a system of vocational education was absolutely necessary to the future welfare of the nation.

While recognizing that training for all the different vocations is important and desirable, agricultural and trade and industrial education are most in need of national encouragement at the present time. The best way to aid the States in giving these kinds of vocational training is through grants for the preparation of efficient teachers and grants for the part payment of their salaries.

National grants are required for the salaries and the training of vocational teachers: (1) To help to solve a problem too large to be worked out extensively and permanently save by the whole nation; (2) to help the States, with their widely varying resources, to carry the cost of giving vocational education and thereby to make this education possible in those States and localities already burdened with the task of meeting the requirements of general education; (3) to equalize among the States the large and unequal task of preparing workers whose tendency to move from State to State is making training for a life work a national as well as a State duty; (4) to give interest and prestige in the States to the work of preparing our youth for useful and productive service.

National grants for agricultural, and trade and industrial education are justified: (1) By the urgency of the demand for the effective training of our workers, which the States can not meet in time without Federal encouragement and aid; (2) by the interstate and national character of the problem, due to its nation-wide interest and importance; (3) by abundant precedent, in appropriations by Congress throughout our entire history, for educational purposes, and in cooperation between the Federal Government and the States, where team play was necessary to handling matters that could not be as well handled by the States alone; (4) by the successful results to the Nation as well as to the States of previous grants for educational purposes.

After six years of consideration of the question by Congress and the country an overwhelming public sentiment favors national grants. The favorable opinions given at the hearings and in answer to questions sent out by the commission to educators, employers and employees, and educational, civic, industrial, agricultural, and commercial organizations national in their scope, were practically unanimous.

The States are facing many new and difficult questions in connection with the efforts to develop agricultural, trade and industrial, commercial, and home economics education. One of the most valuable ways in which the National Government could aid the States in this work would be by national grants expended through Federal agencies for studies, investigations, and reports furthering the efforts of the States to place the work of their vocational schools on a scientific and business-like basis. As a Nation we are singularly lacking in this kind of information. European countries have gained much advantage over us because they are already in possession of this knowledge.

This help can best be secured from the Government. We can not rely upon individuals or national organizations to gather it. The States can not well deal individually with the matter. The work must be done by the National Government to secure the best results. If the Government makes grants to be expended in cooperation with the States for the benefit of any kind of vocational education, every consideration requires that the moneys expended in the venture should be accompanied with all the helpful knowledge that the Federal Government has gleaned or can glean from its studies.

While excellent work has been done by the different Federal agencies in furnishing information and advice to the country for vocational education, the service has been very greatly hampered by a lack of funds. There has to some extent been a lack of close, intimate cooperation between the different departments and bureaus in gathering and using the material. There seems to be more or less overlapping and duplication of effort, not conducive to the best results.

Not only are additional funds needed for the purpose of giving to the States the country-wide sources of information for vocational education in the most effective manner, but some of the Government departments should be organized in some way into a clearing house for the purpose of dealing collectively with the task, so as to have a clear understanding of the respective place and function of each department and bureau and the ways by which they can best cooperate in making their material of the greatest benefit to the States.

RECOMMENDATIONS

I. *Scope of the grants*

1. That national grants be given to the States for the purpose of stimulating vocational education in agriculture and in the trades and industries.

2. That grants be given in two forms:

a. For the training of teachers of agricultural, trade and industrial, and home economics subjects.

b. For the paying of part of the salaries of teachers, supervisors, and directors of agricultural subjects and of teachers of trade and industrial subjects.

3. That appropriations be made to a Federal board for making studies and investigations which shall be of use in vocational schools.

II. *Amount of the grants*

1. For the salaries of teachers, supervisors, and directors of agricultural subjects—that there be appropriated to the States the sum of $500,000 for the fiscal year 1915-16; this amount to be increased at the rate of $250,000 a year until a total of $2,000,000 is reached in the fiscal year 1921-22, and thereafter the annual increase to be at the rate of $500,000 a year until a total maximum appropriation of $3,000,000 is reached in 1923-24.

2. For the salaries of teachers of trade and industrial subjects—that there be appropriated to the States the sum of $500,000 for the fiscal year 1915-16; this annual amount being increased for each subsequent year in the same manner as the grants for the teachers of agricultural subjects, until the same maximum of $3,000,000 is reached in 1923-24.

3. For the training of teachers of agricultural, trade and industrial, and home economics subjects—that there be appropriated to the States the sum of $500,000 for the fiscal year 1915-16; $700,000 for the fiscal year 1916-17; $900,000 for the fiscal year 1917-18; $1,000,000 for the fiscal year 1918-19, and annually thereafter.

4. For the work of the Federal Bureau for Vocational Education—that there be appropriated $200,000 annually, this money to be used in administering the grants to the States and in furnishing information and advice to the States for use in vocational schools and classes.

The maximum in each case above is continued annually thereafter.

III. *Kinds of schools aided by grants*

1. That the schools aided in part by the National Government should be schools supported and controlled by the public.

2. That the education given in these schools should be of less than college grade.

3. That they should be designed to prepare boys and girls over 14 years of age for useful or profitable employment in agriculture and in the trades and industries.

4. That the schools should be of three types in order to meet a variety of needs:

   a. All-day schools in which practically half of the time should be given to actual practice for a vocation on a useful or productive basis.

   b. Part-time schools for young workers over 14 years of age, which should extend either their vocational knowledge or give preparation for entrance to a vocation or extend the general civic or vocational intelligence of the pupils.

   c. Evening schools to extend the vocational knowledge for mature workers over 16 years of age.

IV. *Administration*

1. That the States, in order to receive national grants for vocational education, designate or create State boards, through whom the National Government would deal; the determination of such boards to be left entirely to the States.

2. That a Federal board be created, consisting of the Postmaster General, the Secretary of the Interior, the Secretary of Agriculture, the Secretary of Commerce, and the Secretary of Labor, with the Commissioner of Education as its executive officer, to administer the funds and to cooperate with the States in promoting vocational education.

V. *Conditions*

1. That the Federal statute providing for national grants to the States for vocational education set up conditions safeguarding the proper expenditure of the

money for the purposes designed and insuring a minimum degree of efficiency in the work.

2. That the States, through their legislative authorities, formally accept the conditions of the Federal statute providing national grants.

3. That the States provide for the proper custody and disbursement of the Federal grants allotted to them.

4. That the State board, with the approval of the Federal Board for Vocational Education, formulate plans for the administration of the grants in conformity with the provisions of the Federal statute, and establish minimum requirements for the State as to the qualification of teachers and the equipment of schools.

5. That for each dollar paid from Federal grants allotted to any State for the salaries of vocational teachers, or for the training of vocational teachers, the State or local community, or both, shall expend an equal amount for the same purpose, and shall in addition meet all other costs of plant, equipment, and maintenance, including the salaries of all teachers necessary to complete well-rounded courses of instruction.

6. That the State receive its allotment annually so long as it uses the funds allotted to it in conformity with the purposes and provisions of the Federal statute. Payment on allotments shall be made quarterly.

14

The Return to the Book

ALEXANDER MEIKLEJOHN

One of the most significant exchanges between college and university educators and adult educators has been of ideas about the use of the book as the primary educator of all. Colleges, of course, have long made extensive use of the object known as the textbook; and adult educators have put enormous energy into the preparation of special instructional "literature." Both, however—each stimulating the other—have been active, especially since the 1920s, in promoting what might be called the return to the book, *not the pseudo-book which is so often but a dubious crutch of pedagogy, but the book as a respected and traditional vehicle of adult discourse, whether an acknowledged classic from times past or a recent work of force and distinction. A very early plea for a return to the book in adult education was that delivered to an American Library Association Conference in 1924 by Alexander Meiklejohn. This address, delivered after a good deal of thought had already been given to how best to return to the book but before much had been written about the matter, contains essential ideas which were never abandoned by Meiklejohn, and were later embodied in growing numbers of programs in both college and adult education, to the great enrichment of both.*

I think America, more than anything else, and more than any other nation that ever existed, is a vision, a spiritual adventure, a desire for something better, a purpose, an inspiration, a determination, an enterprise into which a hundred million people have thrown themselves. And I don't believe you can understand America unless you interpret it in those terms.

It is what America wants to be, what she intends to be, what she is determined to be, what she is leading the whole world toward being. That is what you have to think of when you try to understand anything in America. I believe that America intends to be and must be a democracy. That is our mission, that is what we are living for, that is our opportunity.

What is a democracy? As I understand it a democracy is a community which is committed to the principle that every person who comes into our human society is to have, just so far as we can bring it about, an equal opportunity with every other for what life has to give. How is it going to be brought about that every young person shall have a chance at life? You cannot give people very much in the way of living by giving them external things. And to give men votes without understanding is sheer futility.

My theory of democracy is this: Democracy is education. There is only one thing a people can give to its citizens safely. There is only one thing a community can give to its members on a large scale and do it successfully, so far as I know, and that is education. In so far as we can educate the people, in so far as we can bring people to understanding of themselves and of their world we can have a democracy. In so far as we cannot do that we have got to have control by the few.

Can a hundred million people be educated? When I say educated, I mean by that something above the level to which the liberal college goes at present. The question we are facing today is: How far can we go in the process of giving genuine understanding of human living, of making an intelligent society which can understand and control its own affairs? Epictetus summed it all up a couple of thousand years ago when he said: "The rulers of the State have said that only free men shall be educated; but God has said that only educated men shall be free."

From that point of view education in America has not begun. If we are going to have a free people we have got to have a school system in the face of which our present system is a mere beginning. But supposing that a democracy has its people pretty well on the road to education, how is it going to get its thinking done? We have got to find out how a hundred million people can think together on the same question and make their thoughts fit into one another's thoughts in such a way that taken together they shall make sense as a total judgment.

An individual mind is a thing that relates, that unifies, that makes many into one meaning. But when you think of the social mind you find yourself in the presence of a thing which as contrasted with the individual mind, seems to have the structure of a jelly-fish; just a great mass of stuff with no coherent relations, with no nervous system, with no connecting tissues, just many, many multiplicities of difficulty and impulse and no order. We have got to learn intellectual interchange, so that out of a hundred million minds by some way or other, by some scheme or other, one mind, the mind of America may be made.

We are just at the beginning of the greatest adventure of the human spirit. We are going to find a way of thinking together as a people. We won't any longer have people dividing into the two groups, those who think and those who do not, those who decide and those who obey, those who lead and those who follow, those who are spiritual and those who are not. We are going to find our way into the genuine life of a spiritual democracy.

Well, where are our instruments? They are the instruments of intellectual interchange, the newspaper, the magazine, the book and speech. What can we do with the newspaper and the magazine and the book to make many minds into one? That, I think, is our problem.

I think the most obvious characteristic of the graduate of the American college, the most striking and universal characteristic of the graduate of the American college, is that he does not read books. He has read his books. He has been educated. Why is it that the graduates of our colleges are not, as I have been using the term, educated men? I for one have come to the conclusion that the trouble is with our method of instruction. We are trying to communicate knowledge by means of speech, by means of instruction by lectures.

I think we have got to stop it and begin our instruction by reading. In my opinion that is the only funda mental method of instruction. I should, of course, add discussion, but I should make even that secondary.

The process of teaching is the process in which two students go together to the great minds that the human race possesses and try together to get from those minds statements of the problems which will make it possible for them to work out solutions for themselves.

Another great difficulty in the college and school just now is that we are trying to give education to the children of an uneducated people. We are trying to educate in the school when every influence outside the school runs counter to our process. We are trying to make boys and girls in the school read the sort of things that nobody outside the school or college is reading. We are trying to get reading done in a society that does not read. And my own opinion is that the life of a democracy, in one of its definitions at least, could be stated in these terms: A people can be a democracy if it can learn to read, if it can learn to get the wealth that there is in store in the literature of the race, if it can learn to weld itself together into a single intellectual society by the interchange of reading; if it can find present expression for its own meaning and find the record of past meaning. I don't believe that any society can be a democracy in any considerable measure at all except as it develops reading.

I want to see every agency which we can bring to bear in America at work for the education of our older people. We want the workmen educated. We want the owners of property educated. We want parents educated. We want everybody educated. Everything that can be done in America for the education of our people must be done. And those who are in charge of the books seem to me to be at the strategic point.

15

Adult Education: Whose Responsibility?

PRESIDENT'S COMMISSION ON HIGHER EDUCATION

Where responsibility for adult education should rest is an open question in the United States and always has been. It seems unlikely that exclusive responsibility will ever be located at any single point in society but there is nevertheless a wide acceptance of the idea that our higher educational institutions should assume a large role in the activity. This idea was firmly implanted by those great university presidents who devised the rationale for the state universities. A classic statement of the responsibility of colleges and universities was made in the report, Higher Education for American Democracy, *of the President's Commission on Higher Education, 1947. Implicit in this statement is the theory that in modern America the adult education needed is mostly of college level or better, a position which found expression earlier in the Chautauqua movement, but which is by no manner of means yet universally accepted. It can, however, be suggested that adult education should always be at a level higher than the average level of formal education attained by the clients. If this be true, then all worth-while adult education is a variety of higher education for the people concerned and should be so approached by leaders and participants alike.*

The continuing education of the adult population is carried on by many agencies, by some as a deliberate aim, by others as a byproduct not always recognized as education. But the colleges and universities are the best equipped of all the agencies, from the standpoint of resources, to undertake the major part of the job. Education on a near adult level is their business, and they have, in some measure at least, the necessary teachers and facilities.

The present status of university extension services makes it painfully clear that the colleges and universities do not recognize adult education as their potentially greatest service to democratic society. It is pushed aside as something quite extraneous to the real business of the university.

This attitude is fostered by the necessities of adult education. It takes place outside regular college hours and usually off campus. It makes use of faculty members in other units of the university, and for these men extension or correspondence courses are usually extra chores they agree to add to their regular teaching load in order to supplement their inadequate incomes. In this frame of mind, many of them candidly get by with as little expenditure of energy as possible.

This state of affairs cannot be permitted to continue. The colleges and universities should elevate adult education to a position of equal importance with any other of their functions. The extension department should be charged with the task of channeling the resources of every teaching unit of the institution into the adult program.

Adult education, along with undergraduate and graduate education, should become the responsibility of every department or college of the university. It should be the duty of the English faculty or the physics faculty, for instance, to teach English or physics not just to those who come to the campus, but to everyone in the community or the State who wants to learn, or can be persuaded to want to learn, English or physics.

To this degree every college and university should

become a "community college." Then extension teaching would be accounted a part of the regular teaching load and would receive its due share of faculty energy and interest.

Granted that this would increase the job of the institution many times over, that it would require more teachers, more manpower in administration, and a very considerable increase in the budget. The principal obstacle to acceptance of the program, nonetheless, is the limited concept that higher education still holds of its role in a free and democratic society.

It must broaden that concept. It must cease to be campus-bound. It must take the university to the people wherever they are to be found and by every available and effective means for the communication of ideas and the stimulation of intellectual curiosity. It must not hold itself above using all the arts of persuasion to attract consumers for the service it offers.

Adult education in the past has been much too inflexible, much too bound by traditional notions of proper educational procedures. Extension activities for years have been stultified by the idea that adult education consists merely of the transmission to mature people of campus courses developed to meet the needs of adolescents.

Fitting Method to Student

Adult students are not conscript classes. Already established as wage earners, most of them, they do not have to go to school; they have a wide range of activities from which to choose a way of spending their leisure. And adult education is, in most cases, a leisure time activity. The students come to the class or the correspondence lesson at the end of a full and probably tiring day. They want release from the tension of their jobs. They appreciate a much greater degree of informality in atmosphere and method than characterizes most campus classroom teaching.

The program of adult education must be fitted in content, methods, and aims to the adult student as he is, not as the college or the professor thinks he should be.

If adult students are to remain in the class, once enrolled, they must be stimulated and interested. There is nothing to prevent them from dropping a course that does not interest or benefit them, nothing to prevent them from walking out on a teacher who is dull, rambling, and irrelevant.

Adult interest in further education is not predominantly vocational. Many enroll in extension courses to fit themselves for a better job, but many others are motivated by a desire, often vague and fumbling, for self-improvement, which they think a course in literature or history or current events should give them. The majority of them will demand substance in the lecture or the discussion but they will not suffer gladly much academic or specialist jargon.

Vigorous Experimentation

Courses by extension or by correspondence may not be the best means of educating adults; they certainly are not the only ones. Vigorous experimentation with new methods, however unorthodox, is called for.

With the demonstration constantly before us of the appeal and the effectiveness of motion pictures, higher education has been inexcusably slow in the development of visual education. That documentary and educational films could become teaching instruments of great power cannot be doubted. They are becoming so in the elementary and secondary schools.

But all too often the visual education department of the university is relegated to the status of a self-supporting service enterprise, along with the cafeteria or the bookstore, instead of being recognized as a vital educational unit worthy of a substantial budget and the encouragement of administration favor and interest. If use in the adult program brings visual education into its own, all of higher education will benefit.

The great influx of students into the universities and colleges immediately after the war has given much impetus to the development of visual education and other technical aids to learning. The considerable divergence in reading skills and achievement on the part of the students has made it necessary to find devices which make the teacher's presentation more vivid. The greater number of students per teacher and the lack of preparation on the part of many new teachers has augmented the need for effective training aids.

The experiences of the armed forces in World War II afford an excellent example for institutions of higher learning as they cope with the problems of mass education. During the war the service's training schools were faced with the necessity of evolving effective and rapid methods for mass instruction. With a practically unlimited budget they made marvelous strides in the development of motion pictures, strip films, transcriptions, mock-ups and other learning devices. The primary and successful application of these devices to wartime training purposes suggests the need for further exploration in an effort to develop similar devices for peacetime academic instruction.

There are currently certain handicaps to an extensive development of the use of technical aids at the college level. Primarily the meagerness of existing materials available for use in higher educational instruction retards this development. There is also a lack of information and centralized distribution of such materials as are presently in existence. Several institutions, notably Rutgers, Pennsylvania State College, the State University of Iowa, and Vassar, have developed effective materials for their own use. Doubtless these materials would have wider application and use in other institutions if a procedure for interchange of information and actual materials were developed.

This Commission recommends the establishment of a continuing committee devoted to the study, development, and utilization of technical aids to learning in higher education.

Such a committee should deal with four major areas of responsibility. In the first place, it should provide facilities for coordinating information on existing materials and develop a plan for the interchange of these materials among interested institutions. Secondly, the Committee should arrange for continued study of the special devices developed by the Navy, Army, and Air Corps to discover possible applications these developments may have for civilian instruction. Another important activity would be the stimulation of individual institutions or groups of institutions in a program of integrated effort at developing further basic-training aids. This committee should also assume responsibility for wide publicity on the advantages and objectives of technical aids in higher education.

The Commission is of the opinion that the work of such a committee would be most effective by having it attached to some existing educational organization which has sufficient prestige to challenge the serious consideration of institutions of higher education.

University owned and operated radio stations are another agency for adult education whose possibilities are all too seldom exploited. Their influence and appeal where they exist is widespread.

Yet here again the universities are niggardly and slow. The Federal Communications Commission has set aside twenty bands on the FM spectrum for the use of educational institutions, but the colleges are not taking advantage of the opportunity thus offered them. They are repeating the mistake they made twenty years ago when they failed to take up the channels reserved for them in the AM spectrum. The FCC cannot be expected to hold out against the pressure of commercial interests that want these FM bands if the colleges and universities show no interest in making use of them.

Objectives of Adult Education

Whatever methods may prove best for reaching and instructing large numbers of the adult population, the purposes of the program are in large measure those of higher education in general. The adult program is not an additional objective of the college; it is one of the means by which the college can achieve its general objectives.

The knowledge, attitudes, and activities necessary for responsible citizenship in our free society cannot be left to the oncoming generation; they are needed now. The urgent necessities of world-wide understanding and cooperation cannot be postponed until the insight and good will on which they depend have been developed in a new generation; they call for thought and action now.

Higher education will not play its social role in American democracy and in international affairs successfully unless it assumes the responsibility for a program of adult education reaching far beyond the campus and the classroom.

16

Toward National Organization

AMERICAN ASSOCIATION FOR ADULT EDUCATION AND ADULT EDUCATION ASSOCIATION OF THE U.S.A.

Adult education, since it is concerned with the education of people deeply immersed in the exacting business of living, is inherently a widely dispersed activity, diverse in content, method, and short- and long-term objectives. Nevertheless it must be presumed also to have a common element, the perception and acknowledgment of which will cue all hands to join an organization designed to embrace the complexity. Although several special adult education programs attained during their histories something approaching national coverage, notably the lyceums and Chautauqua, it was not until 1925 that the first effort to construct a comprehensive national organization covering the whole dispersed field was made. This organization lasted a quarter-century and was immediately succeeded by another with the same essential aim. By looking at the "objects" of these organizations we get an idea of the state of self-consciousness and sense of direction characteristic at the moments they were launched.

CONSTITUTION OF THE AMERICAN ASSOCIATION FOR ADULT EDUCATION

(Adopted at Cleveland, Ohio, October 17, 1925)

ARTICLE I—*Name*

The name of the association shall be "The American Association for Adult Education."

ARTICLE II—*Object*

Its object shall be to promote the development and improvement of adult education in the United States and to cooperate with similar associations in other countries. It shall undertake to provide for the gathering and dissemination of information concerning adult education aims and methods of work; to keep its members informed concerning the achievements and problems of adult education in other countries; to conduct a continuous study of work being done in this field and to publish from time to time the results of such study; to respond to public interest in adult education and to cooperate in the formation of study groups whether within or without regular educational institutions; to cooperate with organizations and individuals engaged in educational work of this nature in the task of securing books and instructors; and to serve in such other ways as may be deemed advisable.

CONSTITUTION OF THE ADULT EDUCATION ASSOCIATION OF THE UNITED STATES OF AMERICA

(Adopted at Columbus, Ohio, May 14, 1951)

PREAMBLE

In the belief that only a vigorous, informed, and democratically vigilant people can remain free—

In the recognition that among a free people learning for every citizen must be a process continuing throughout life—

In the understanding that the capacity to perfect skills, to enrich living, and to increase social understanding and effectiveness is ever present in human beings—

In the knowledge that adult education must seek continuously new and better ways to achieve these ends and ideals—

We, who share these convictions, seek to build a stronger adult education movement through the creation of this association.

ARTICLE I—*Name*

The name of this Association shall be "The Adult Education Association of the United States of America."

ARTICLE II—*Purpose*

The purpose of the Association shall be to further the concept of education as a process continuing throughout life by affording to educators of adults and to other interested persons opportunities to increase their competence, by encouraging organizations to develop adult education activities and to work together in the interests of adult education, by receiving and disseminating educational information, by promoting the balanced development of educational services needed by the adult population in the United States, and by cooperating with adult education agencies internationally.

Sources

1. Cotton Mather. *Essays to do Good: Addressed to All Christians, Whether in Public or Private Capacities.* Originally published 1710. Edition used: Boston, 1808.
2. Benjamin Franklin. *Autobiography.* Originally published in America 1818, first complete edition 1867. Edition used: Collector's Edition.
3. Timothy Claxton. *Memoir of a Mechanic,* Boston, 1839.
4. The Lyceums. See *Old South Leaflets,* Vol. VI, pp. 126-150. Originally published, Boston, 1829.
5. John Lowell, Jr. Text supplied by Mr. Ralph Lowell, May 22, 1958.
6. Edward Everett and George Ticknor. The Everett letter is quoted in various volumes dealing with the history of libraries in America (but is *not* quoted in the life of Everett by Frothingham!). The Ticknor letter is to be found in *Life, Letters and Journals of George Ticknor* by George S. Hillard, Boston, 1876.
7. Peter Cooper. Here reprinted from a pamphlet (not copyrighted) entitled *Charter and Trust Deed* of the Cooper Union. Originally published 1881. Edition used: 1951.
8. John Heyle Vincent. *The Chautauqua Movement,* Boston, 1886.
9. W. R. Harper. Quoted in *The Chautauqua Movement,* Boston, 1886.
10. Thomas Davidson. *The Education of Wage Earners,* papers by Davidson, edited by Charles M. Bakewell. Boston: Ginn & Company, 1904.
11. University Education. The selection reproduces the larger part of the text of *Ten Years Report of the American Society for the Extension of University Teaching 1890-1900,* Philadelphia, 1901.

12. Lester Ward. *Applied Sociology: a Treatise on the Conscious Improvement of Society by Society.* Boston, 1906.
13. Rationale of Vocational Education. The text is the "Summary" of *The Report of the Commission on National Aid to Vocational Education,* House Document 1004, 63d Congress, 2d Session. Washington: Government Printing Office, 1914.
14. Alexander Meiklejohn. Selection is an edited version of an abstract of an extemporaneous speech published in *Bulletin of the American Library Association,* Vol. 18, No. 4-A. *Papers and Proceedings, Saratoga Springs Conference, 1924.* Chicago, 1924.
15. Adult Education: Whose Responsibility? Selection is a passage from *Higher Education for American Democracy,* A Report of the President's Commission on Higher Education, Vol. I. Washington: Government Printing Office, 1947.
16. Toward National Organization. The 1925 AAAE constitution in full is to be found in Carnegie Corporation, Office Memorandum, November 23, 1925, Series II, Adult Education, Number 15; Digest of Proceedings of National Conference on Adult Education, Cleveland, Ohio, October 16-17, 1925. The 1951 AEA constitution in full is to be found in *Adult Education* (a magazine), Vol. I, No. 5, June 1951.